This book contains a treasure tro
practical exercises. It successfully ....,. ....
teachings and indicates how these are relevant and applicable today. Within these pages you will be delighted by the masterful arrangement of such topics as cultivating gratitude, giving and receiving love and creating a sense of well-being in your life. The book also provides a series of simple, enjoyable yet powerful exercises that can be easily incorporated into your daily life.

Dr Melanie Chan, author of:
Life Coaching - Life Changing, O-Books.
Contemporary Representations of Virtual Reality. New York, Continuum.

Every major faith tradition urges us to live by the Golden Rule: to be to others as we would wish them to be to us. They often fall short, however, in giving practical help in actually doing this. Spiritual self-help books, on the other hand, may give us practical guidance but often lack real spiritual substance. In 'The Tree of Becoming' Trevor Morris has very effectively addressed both the ideal and the practice of living from a centre of love.

Margaret Silf, author of:
Landmarks: Exploration of Ignatian Spirituality
Landscapes of Prayer: Finding God in the World and Your Life
One Hundred Wisdom Stories: From Around the World
The Other Side of Chaos: Breaking Through
When Life is Breaking Down

The Tree of Becoming

A Guide to the Seven Principles of Conscious Healing and Transformation

Ann
May your life be full
of light and love

Trevor

X

TREVOR MORRIS

ISBN: 978-1-4834-5054-4 (sc)
ISBN: 978-1-4834-5055-1 (e)

Library of Congress Control Number: 2014920852

Because of the dynamic nature of the Internet, any web addresses or links contained in
this book may have changed since publication and may no longer be valid. The views
expressed in this work are solely those of the author and do not necessarily reflect the
views of the publisher, and the publisher hereby disclaims any responsibility for them.

Lulu Publishing Services rev. date: 4/7/2016

Contents

Conscious healing and transformation
The creative process
The seven principles of conscious healing and transformation
Affirmations
My magic box
The tree of becoming

The first principle of conscious healing and transformation

See and feel love and beauty around you
Accept people and things as they are
Welcome adversity in your life
Give spontaneously
Radiate love
Learn to receive love
Nurture your inner child
Forgive other people in your life
Look after your body
Be strong
Affirmations: create love in your life

Write your vision statement
Draw your tree of becoming
Let go of resistance to your vision
Create a mental movie
Re-dream your day
Fake it until you make it
Attract the money you need
Attract your soul mate
Attract work that you like
Heal yourself using the power of your mind
Stay young
Be positive
Offer up your vision in prayer
Important cautionary note
Affirmations: create your vision for the future

Recognise recurring patterns in your life
Be aware of the metaphors you use
Plant your new beliefs in your unconscious mind
Let go of damaging thoughts and emotions
Face up to your addictions
Improve your relationships
Do small things to show that you care
Welcome new relationships
Learn how to resolve conflict
Go to new places

Break the chains that bind you
Welcome change
Affirmations: change habits that chain you to the past

The sixth principle of conscious healing and transformation

Create an action plan
Act selflessly
Be persistent
Look for good role models
Network
Declutter your life
Seize the moment
Release your fears
Use your emotions; don't let them use you
Transform your anger
Create emotional anchors
Tread gently
Turn crisis into opportunity
Listen to the whispers
Affirmations: put your dreams into action

The seventh principle of conscious healing and transformation

Celebrate this moment
Be grateful
Praise people
Celebrate friendships
Play and have fun
Come together and celebrate

Keep a diary of your progress
Rise above difficult times in your life
Celebrate beginnings
Celebrate endings
Raise your spirit in prayer
Affirmations: enjoy and celebrate life

Acupuncture
Aromatherapy
Changing your beliefs
Cognitive behavioural therapy (CBT)
Emotional freedom technique (EFT)
5Rhythms
Friends
Homeopathy
Ho'oponopono
Mindfulness meditation
Modern herbalism
Neuro-linguistic programming (NLP)
Spiritual help
Subliminal suggestion
Vital energy

Reflections on health
Reflections on destiny and fate
Reflections on the Sri Yantra
Reflections on enlightenment and the kingdom of heaven
Reflections on the ego

Reflections on the nature of God
Reflections on time and space
Reflections on universal truths

List of Practical Exercises

Acknowledgements

This book is the result of my personal experience. Many people have helped me on my journey towards a better understanding of life. They have given me a firm belief in our oneness with each other and our oneness with the divine spark within us all.

I would like to thank the following people in particular:

Joy for her love and support, and for reminding me of the hypocrisy of so much that purports to be spiritual in the world in which we live.

Gavin Whyte for conscientiously editing my initial manuscript and providing valuable advice on content and presentation.

Jenny Smith and Jean Patrickson for their observations and corrections to my final manuscript.

Karen Rose Ramsay for her suggestions and amendments to the section on 5Rhythms.

Donna Taylor for her constant support and encouragement and for our many discussions about the processes outlined in this book.

Michelle Finlay for her inspiration for the tree illustrations used in this book.

Melanie Chan and Margaret Silf for supporting me in the publication of this book.

Individual clients who have shared with me their personal experiences, from whom I have learned so much. Thank you for the trust you have placed in me.

Alan Bamford for his guidance on our journey towards discovering the light that shines within us all.

Preface

The One remains, the many change and pass
Heaven's light forever shines, Earth's shadows fly
Life, like a dome of many-coloured glass
Stains the white radiance of eternity
Until death tramples it to fragments.

*Percy Bysshe Shelley, Adonais, an elegy on the
death of Keats.*

CHAPTER 1:
Introduction

Conscious healing and transformation

The purpose of this book is to help you become who you truly are. It is about manifesting your spiritual being and radiating love and abundance to others. When you are being yourself you will know intuitively what to do in order to become fulfilled in your life. You will attract happiness and fulfilment to yourself and to those around you. Once you are doing things from a *place of being* you will automatically attract the things you need.

The principles outlined in Chapters 2 to 8 of this book will help you to do the following things:

- Discover your unique identity and purpose in life and your connection to the universal love that pervades all creation.
- Attract what you need to create true and lasting happiness for yourself and others around you.
- Increase your self-confidence and self-esteem.
- Improve your vitality and health.
- Make positive changes affecting your work, money and relationships.
- Break through blockages and negative patterns that restrict your enjoyment of life.
- Find true happiness based upon love for yourself and all creation.

The creative process

Many people believe they need to *have* things, in order to *do* things that will make them happy, in order to *be* the person they want to be. However, the creative process works exactly the opposite way. First, you need to *be* connected to your true self, that is one with universal love, and then you need to *do* things that are consistent with your identity. You will then automatically attract the things you need.

The creative process always follows the following simple process:

$$Be \rightarrow Do \rightarrow Have$$

Who you choose to *be* needs to relate to your spiritual purpose in this life. What you *do* needs to be in harmony with your spiritual purpose and an expression of your own free will.
What you *have* will manifest in the physical dimension as a result of what you choose to be and do.

Transformation takes place spontaneously when your spirit, mind, emotions and physical body are in harmony with one another and directed towards achieving your life's true purpose.

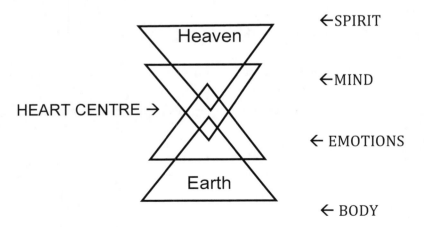

When all aspects of your being are in harmony, creative energy flows naturally from heaven towards earth, and vital energy flows from the earth towards heaven. These two flows of energy are represented in the previous diagram by the downward-pointing and upward-pointing sets of triangles. The two flows of energy meet at your heart centre, where the triangles intersect. This is the centre of your being.

While living on earth, it is helpful to keep a balance between all aspects of your being. For example, you need to manifest your highest spiritual purpose in life and feel love and compassion for others, but at the same time you need to take care of your physical needs.

Unfortunately, most of us have lost this state of harmony. Sometimes, however, we do experience a state of elation and harmony when we feel totally happy and at peace. This often occurs when we experience a feeling of love. This love may be directed towards another person, nature, dancing, swimming, or just about anything. Whatever the love you feel, it will be a reflection of your personality and individuality. This is a natural state of being.

We lose this state of love when we suppress who we really are and develop fear of people and the world around us. Fear is the opposite of love. Fear inevitably leads to unhappiness, and in time it will makes us physically ill. Suppression and fear are often linked to childhood experiences or traumatic events in life. There may also be an inherited component. For example, we may inherit a tendency towards being naturally happy or despondent, or a predisposition to certain types of illness.

The good news is that we can let go of the effects of our previous experience. We can learn to overcome our fears, and to trust people and the world around us. We can manifest our unique personality in our lives. Our lives do not have to be predetermined by our genes or our childhood experiences. Although these are powerful influences in our lives, we have

3

an even greater power to transform these influences - by harnessing our spiritual energy and the power of our conscious mind.

The seven principles of conscious healing and transformation

Create love in your life.
Radiate your own unique light into the world.
Find peace within yourself.
Create your vision for the future.
Change habits that chain you to the past.
Put your dreams into action.
Enjoy and celebrate life.

Chapter 2 to Chapter 8 of this book explain the above principles. If you understand these principles and learn to use them in your everyday life, you will become happy and fulfilled at a deep level of your being.

There is a chapter for each of the seven principles. Each chapter gives a description of the relevant principle and a number of practical exercises. It is important that you carry out the exercises that are relevant for you. Though it is useful to understand the principles, it is more important to put them into practice.

As you follow the principles outlined in this book, you will experience amazing changes in your life. At times, your life may feel almost magical and unreal. You may experience - for the first time - what it is like to be really alive, living in the moment and enjoying the spontaneity of life.

The first three principles involve bringing love into your life and learning how to *be* connected at all times to your true self and universal love. The next four principles deal with the process of manifestation and relate to what you are choosing to *do* in your life.

Being and doing are equally important in your life.

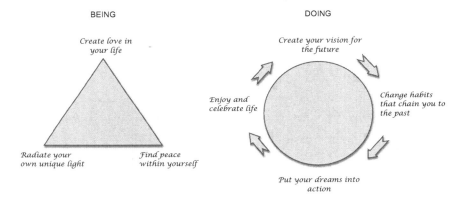

Affirmations

At the end of each of the chapters dealing with the seven principles (two to eight) there is a list of affirmations; these relate to the issues considered in these chapters. They are given as examples of affirmations you might use to help you change your beliefs and attitudes. You can use these, or create your own affirmations using wording and imagery that appeals to you.

Affirmations are concise statements about the way you wish to be and the way you choose to relate to the external world. You would normally keep a list of these somewhere handy and recite them out loud maybe once or twice a day (before you go to sleep would be a good time).

In my experience, affirmations can be very helpful in summarizing the changes you have decided to make in your life and implanting these in your mind. But, used on their own, they have certain limitations. Many people become disheartened when they discover that simply reciting their affirmations does not bring about the changes they desire. For example: if you lack self-confidence you might use the following affirmation:

> Every day I wake up in the morning feeling full of enthusiasm and confident that I can deal with any challenges that the day might bring.

The problem is - if you don't really believe at an unconscious level that you *could* wake up feeling confident, no amount of repeating this affirmation will change the way you feel. This doesn't mean the affirmation is useless - far from it. Used in conjunction with the other advice in this book you will be able to achieve these changes in your life. Using this example: it is important that aside from reciting your affirmation, you begin to take risks and do things in your life that will help you to feel more confident. Once you begin to do this, the unconscious mind will start to accept your affirmation.

My magic box

Throughout this book it is suggested that you keep a record of certain things or file certain information somewhere special. You could use a file that you like, or keep your information in a beautiful folder or box. I like to use a box folder. It is important to keep this information together in one place. I suggest that you keep the following information in your magic box.

- Your affirmations
- A list of things you are grateful for
- Your vision statement
- Your tree of becoming
- Your list of new beliefs

- A list of places you would like to go to
- Your action plan
- Any pictures or poems that you love

The tree of becoming

A tree is a metaphor for growth and development in many cultures of the world. Symbolically, it forms a strong connection between heaven and earth, and it can be used as a powerful archetype for becoming the person you chose to be (in harmony with your spiritual purpose and universal love).

This book is named after Exercise 19, which appears in Chapter 5 of this book. The exercise concerns drawing your tree of becoming. This is a powerful visual image of the changes you are making and the energies you are attracting into your life: changes that will bring happiness into your life and the lives of those around you.

CHAPTER 2:

Create love in your life

The first principle of conscious healing and transformation

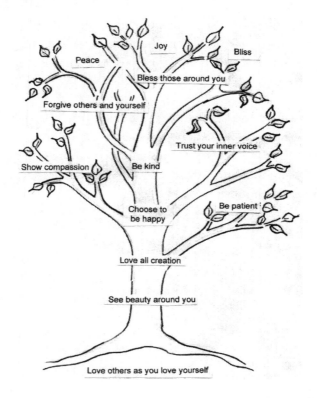

If only we could give a little love each day, to everyone who comes our way.
Apple served with whiskey and spice, or anything that is just as nice.
Love speaks a language all its own: Lithuanian, English, or Unknown.
The Author

Love is the most creative force in the universe. By allowing more love into your life you will automatically attract the things you need to make you happy and bring more happiness to those around you. You may feel there is not enough love in your life and that you have little control over the amount of love that comes your way. But this is not true. You can attract love into your life, but only if you start giving love rather than only expecting to receive it.

If you would like more love in your life, you must start behaving differently. This will change the way other people see you, and more importantly, it will change the way you see yourself. In this chapter, there are some practical exercises that will help you create and radiate love around you. Whatever you wish to change, bringing more love into your life will help you attract the things you need. Bringing love into your life is essential if you wish to transform your life in a creative way.

When we love, we become part of everything around us. We lose our sense of fear and isolation and begin to radiate energy and enthusiasm to those around us. Bringing more love into our lives enables us to overcome subconscious fears and insecurities that are at the root of all unhappiness and serious disease.

Love is closely associated with the heart and the energy needed for the heart to be vigorous and healthy. People who become hard-hearted become vulnerable to illness and depression. The heart is the centre of our being; if the heart is unhealthy, it will affect the whole of our being, leading to serious illness and death.

Love is the emotion that heals the heart. It has three forms of expression:

- Loving and seeing beauty in things around you (the universe).
- Accepting and loving other people without trying to change or manipulate them.
- Accepting and loving yourself exactly as you are.

Love is an attitude. It is about respecting and honouring things as they are. It is the opposite of fear. It is based on the knowledge that everything is exactly as it should be, and that the universe provides for all our needs.

It is our inability to see the whole picture that leads us to believe things are not as they should be. Once we accept things exactly as they are, our lives will change in miraculous ways.

Consider the following Taoist story:

> There was a wise farmer who had worked in the fields for many years. One day, his horse ran away. Upon hearing the news, his neighbours came to visit. *Such bad luck,* they said sympathetically. *Maybe,* the old man replied.
>
> The next morning, the horse returned bringing with it three wild horses. *How wonderful,* his neighbours exclaimed. *Maybe,* replied the old man.
>
> The following day, his son tried to ride one of the untamed horses, but he was thrown of and broke his leg. The neighbours came again. *How unfortunate,* they said. *Maybe,* the old man replied.
>
> The day after, military officials came to the village to draft young men into the army. When they saw that the boy's leg was broken, they passed him by. The neighbours congratulated the farmer. *How well things have turned out,* they said. *Maybe,* the old man replied.

The moral of this story is that a wise person refuses to judge anything that happens. Instead of judging what is, he or she simply accepts what is. He or she knows that it is often impossible to understand what place or purpose a seemingly random event has in the tapestry of life.

Love is always a two-way process. If you start to radiate and give love, you will soon begin to receive love. If you feel there is no love in your life, you need to focus on giving more love to others and yourself.

The more depressed or negative you feel about life, the more essential it is for you to practise giving love to yourself and others. If you see love and beauty around you, your life will become full of love and beauty. If you believe the world is a terrible and frightening place, your life will go from bad to worse. This is the real meaning of heaven and hell. The following table illustrates some of the differences between these two states of being:

HELL = fear and deprivation	HEAVEN = love and abundance
Life is hard and suffering is necessary for personal/spiritual growth.	Life is a beautiful, wonderful and enjoyable experience. Personal and spiritual growth takes place naturally.
People use and take advantage of me.	People want to help me and genuinely care about me.
People don't like me as I am and are out to get me.	People like and accept me when I am true to myself.
Everything in my life is wrong.	Everything in my life is exactly as it is meant to be.
I must do what my family and people expect of me.	I am free to be myself.
It is impossible to change my life.	I can change my life right now.
Life gets worse and worse.	Life gets better and better.
I am worthless.	I am grateful for my life and love myself just the way I am.
I don't deserve to have a good life.	Life is full of joy and fun.

You can choose to be in heaven or hell.

Hell is a state of fear and deprivation; heaven is a state of love and abundance. You either choose to see life as hell, or you choose to see it as heaven. The more you think life is hell, the more it becomes like hell. Your negative attitude attracts negative people and negative situations. You cannot begin the transformation process if you do not believe that good things happen (and that good things can happen for you). It is no good asking if you don't believe you will receive. But don't just sit around and expect these things to turn up. You need to change your behaviour and attitudes. It is not that difficult; simply choose to see the world in a different way.

See and feel love and beauty around you

If you *choose* to see and feel love and beauty around you, it will transform your life - even if you do nothing else. I understand, the more problems you have, the more difficult this will seem at first. But if you try, you will always find some things to love in your life.

Seek and you *will* find the kingdom of heaven. You may keep hearing an inner voice saying, *but it is not true; my life is hard and full of suffering.* Don't try to suppress this voice. Instead, continue to seek out beautiful and positive things in your life.

Exercise 1: See and feel love and beauty around you

Stop where you are right now. What can you see, hear, feel, and touch that is beautiful? Look around you, look out of the window, listen to the wind or the rain, pick up an apple from the fruit dish, or walk on the wet grass with bare feet. Try to get in touch with a childlike sense of wonder.

Discover for yourself the beauty and wonder that is around you. Stretch out and extend your mind and all your senses so that you come into contact with the beautiful things that surround you.

After you have done this, sit down quietly and write down at least three beautiful things in your life. Don't think too hard; just write down things that come to mind or appeal to your senses. Do this exercise once per day for about a week. Compile a list of at least twenty beautiful things in your life. It should only take you about five minutes each day.

See, feel, hear, smell, and touch the beauty and love that surrounds you. Use all your senses, and try to be at one with the beauty and wonder of the universe.

After a week, start to bring this attitude into your daily life. Instead of writing down what you are experiencing, stop for a few minutes during the day to see and feel things that inspire you and make you happy. As you are doing this, feel a sense of gratitude for the wonderful things in your life.

Let this exercise become an automatic part of your life.

There are many ways you can modify this exercise on your own or in groups. For example, you can use drawing, dancing, or singing to express the sense of love and connection you have with people and things around you.

To see a world in a grain of sand and heaven in a wild flower
Hold infinity in the palm of your hand and eternity in an hour.
William Blake, Auguries of Innocence

Accept people and things as they are

Accepting and welcoming people and creatures as they are is a powerful expression of love. We need to give other people and all creatures the opportunity and space to live their own lives. Trying to get people or events to conform to our expectations is not an expression of love; it is an expression of the self-centred ego.

- Allow people to learn in their own way and make their own mistakes.
- Don't tell other people what they should do.
- Recognise good qualities in people and in different cultures.
- Give the best advice you can *only* when you want to help and it is clear that you have knowledge and experience that could be useful.
- Celebrate the fact that other people's lifestyles, culture, and habits are different from yours.
- Do everything you can to protect the habitat and lives of other creatures on the planet (start with the creatures that live near you).
- Be gentle and take care of yourself. Recognise that you have particular strengths (and don't beat yourself up about your weaknesses).
- Accept events that happen in your life that you don't like but are outside of your control (the universe mirrors back to us experiences we need for our greater good). As you develop a greater spiritual understanding you may learn to welcome adversity in your life!

If you condemn or judge things about other people, similar things will be reflected back into your life, until such time as you learn to allow them without judgment. This 'mirror' of what you judge teaches you to allow within others the possibility of thought, action and feeling that you may not allow within yourself. In other words, other people have a freedom to do what they want and you do not have the right to judge their actions.

You may not agree with their actions, but you do not have the right to judge them.

You will discover that, once you stop dictating what should happen in your life and the lives of others, you will become more peaceful. This allows people and things around you to change in a more harmonious way. But this doesn't mean you shouldn't ever try to change things in your life or try to influence things for the better in the world. However, the first thing you must do if you want to change anything is to acknowledge the way things are at the moment, without judging yourself or others. This applies whether you are trying to deal with some form of addiction, anxiety, depression, or sudden outbursts of anger. You will only change this behaviour once you have accepted things as they are without condemning yourself or other people. Learn to separate behaviour from the person who exhibits it. A person's behaviour is not the person. People are inherently good.

Once you understand and accept people or situations as they are - without anger or resentment - you are in a strong position to change things for the better. Change takes place not by condemning behaviour, but by focusing attention on more positive qualities. We do not change a situation by condemning it or the people involved; we change a situation by focusing on a more healthy and loving way of living. For example:

- Fight poverty by helping and supporting people to develop and use their talents and resources.
- Do not condemn or criticise people for antisocial behaviour. Make sure they are aware of the effect their actions have on other people, and then help them identify their positive qualities. After that, find ways to help them to use their talents in a creative way.
- Before trying to change others, be sure that your actions are not partly responsible for their behaviour.

- Recognise and accept that a problem exists before it becomes a crisis. Deal with the issues. How many riots or wars are caused by unresolved grievances or inequalities that are ignored or pushed under the carpet?
- If you are not sure what to do in any situation: accept things are the way they are, be still for a few moments, and say to yourself, *what would a wise and compassionate person do in this situation?* You will usually get a clear answer within moments, or if not, within a short space of time.

Always remember that what you resist persists. Wars usually lead to more wars, and more people get dragged into the conflict. Even when wars come to an end, they leave a legacy of suffering, anger, and hatred that may take generations to resolve. In the end, mutual understanding and compassion need to be reached. We need to accept each other's existence and find ways to live and work together. Love is a more powerful force than fear, and a primary expression of love is unconditional acceptance of people and things as they are.

Accepting people or events as they are, is not the same as doing nothing. Acceptance is the foundation stone for appropriate action. There are situations in life where strong action is justified - to protect people who are being abused and to modify the behaviour of people responsible for abuse. This intervention may involve the use of limited force, the application of sanctions, or the setting of rules that affect people's behaviour. Often, we need to set boundaries when dealing with damaging relationships. In a wider sense, these actions are all forms of love because they encourage people to change in a positive way. A key thing to remember is that it is useless to bury your head in the sand and pretend that a problem does not exist. First, recognise and accept that a problem exists. After that, set a clear intention to change the situation in the best interest of all concerned.

Strong action should always be motivated by a genuine intention to help all involved. The use of force for personal gain or power can never be justified. Underlying all forceful action should be a clear intention of compassion and love.

Love the animals, love the plants, love everything. If you love everything, you will perceive the divine mystery in things. Once you perceive it, you will begin to comprehend it better every day. And you will come at last to love the whole world with an all-embracing love.
Fyodor Dostoyevsky

Welcome adversity in your life

One less understood aspect of love is welcoming with good grace everything that comes into your life. It is easy to welcome the good things in your life, but welcoming the bad things is a powerful key to transforming your life. What we welcome has the potential to be transformed; what we resist persists.

Accept and welcome the following things:

- Difficulties and adversity
- Physical and mental illness
- Loneliness
- Your failings and addictions
- Other people you instinctively dislike

All these things have a purpose. Pain and suffering exist to help us learn to change. The more we resist change, the more we suffer. If we burn ourselves, the pain teaches us not to repeat that action. It is the same with all pain - physical, emotional, and psychological. Pain and suffering are messages to learn from experience.

Your experience of life is exactly what your higher self has chosen for your growth and development. Your spirit knows why you have chosen this life; everything in your life is exactly as it is meant to be. Once you accept this amazing fact, your life will begin to transform itself.

Exercise 2: Welcome adversity

Learn by heart the following sentence, and whenever you feel unhappy or depressed, say it out loud:

Everything that is happening now is for my greater good. I am learning from this experience, and I am ready to accept any changes I need to make in order to be happy and fulfilled.

Once you have said this, try to focus on what you are doing in this instant. Be determined to find some satisfaction or joy in whatever is happening. Look for the good things that can come out of your situation, and shift your attention away from your negative feelings.

At first, you may find this difficult, but the more you practise this exercise, the easier it will become. Eventually, you will be able to face all difficult situations in your life and transform them into useful experiences.

Kites rise highest against the wind.
Winston Churchill

Give spontaneously

Most of us give presents at festivals and other special occasions, such as birthdays. This is fine, but it is not always done in the true spirit of giving; at times, finding a suitable present becomes an unwelcome chore.

Real love is unconditional and spontaneous. It is about all the little things that you do selflessly for others. A spontaneous smile given with no ulterior motive is a true act of love. Many of the benefits of unconditional love act at a subtle level of our being. By giving to others, we become connected to the outer world; our ego becomes less important, and we become less attached to ourselves. This creates a state of happiness and contentment that cannot be achieved by only striving to increase our own wellbeing or possessions.

Exercise 3: Give spontaneously

Make a conscious effort to do one special thing for someone every day. The key thing is to deliberately choose to do something that will make someone else happy. That may or may not be something you want to do. Here are some ideas for special things you could do, but remember to put yourself in the other person's shoes. What will make that person happy in this moment?

- Call, e-mail, or visit someone you think may be lonely or having a difficult time.
- Give things spontaneously to friends and people you meet.
- Smile at and imagine sending love to people you like.
- Let people know that you admire or respect them.
- Give to charities that inspire you.
- Feed wildlife such as birds and squirrels.

- Celebrate other people's successes and special occasions.
- Help people who have a problem, especially those who cross your path.
- Show compassion for people who are unhappy or sick.
- Cuddle the cat or the dog.
- Take care of lost or injured birds and animals.
- Wish people well and bless things and people around you.
- Be pleasant to and respect people you meet.
- Be there for people when they are going through a crisis.

Start with small things and spend time thinking about what you can do to make other people happy. You will be amazed how therapeutic this can be.

Composting your vegetables and replenishing the soil are also acts of giving, as is recycling natural resources and consumer items. Make these actions part of your life.

Look out for opportunities to give as they occur. It is a wonderful experience to give spontaneously; it opens the heart and creates a doorway for love to come into your life. Eventually, this becomes an automatic process whereby you give spontaneously to other people and the universe around you. Do not seek recognition or reward. Give for the love of giving and the pleasure you feel in your heart.

A good practice is to give anonymously to people you don't know.

But when thou doest alms, let not thy left hand know what thy right hand doeth.
The Bible (KJV), Matthew 6:3

Radiate love

Radiating love is something you can do all the time. It is about opening your heart to people and things around you. It is about paying attention to what is going on and stretching out to help and support others. This includes developing a caring and loving attitude towards animals and the environment. By doing this, you build up a relationship with things around you and break down barriers that exist between you and the outer world.

Developing this attitude will promote your health and well-being. Many illnesses are caused by fear of relationships with others and the belief that things in our environment can hurt us. That is not to say that we can't be hurt by bad relationships or environmental pollution, but quite often, our anger and fears do more damage than what we are afraid of. When we radiate love to others, we overcome fear and flood our bodies with healing chemicals such as endorphins.

The more you radiate love freely into the world the more love you will attract into your life. Paradoxically, however, for this to happen you should never give love with the intention of receiving anything in return. In general, whatever feelings you radiate into the world will be reflected back into your life in some way. For example: if you feel angry, bitter or unloving to others, these feelings will be reflected in the behaviour of people appearing in your life. This 'mirror' of what you radiate to others teaches you to be mindful of your thoughts, emotions and actions at any particular time, and the effect these are having on people (and other conscious beings) in your life.

Exercise 4: Radiate love

Imagine a time when you felt totally happy and at one with the world. This might have been when you were deeply in love or a time when you were able to fully express yourself. Whatever the situation, imagine how you felt at that time and allow yourself to experience the same sense of enchantment, ecstasy, and peace. Now imagine that you are radiating this feeling from the area of your heart to people and the world around you. Allow this feeling to expand and encompass things that you meet.

You may wish to compose a short affirmation that you say to yourself or out loud that expresses the feelings you are radiating. This needs to be something that comes from the depth of your inner being. It should reflect who you are and the unique nature of the love and beauty that you are giving to people and the world around you.

Imagine these feelings as often as possible during the day. You don't necessarily need to direct these feelings to any particular person or with any particular intent, although you may do so if the feelings genuinely come from your heart. If you want to help a particular person who is suffering, send him or her unconditional love and imagine the person connected to a beautiful spiritual light above their head.

The heart generates the body's most powerful and most extensive rhythmic electromagnetic field. Compared to the electric field produced by the brain, the heart's electric field is about sixty times greater in amplitude, and it permeates every cell in the body. The heart's magnetic field is approximately five thousand times stronger than the brain's magnetic field.

Radiate boundless love towards the entire world
Above, below, and across
Unhindered, without ill will, without enmity
The Buddha, Keraniya Metta Sutta: The discourse on loving kindness

Learn to receive love

Lack of self-love is why some people are always giving to others but find it difficult to receive or attract love themselves. When we love and accept ourselves, we no longer need to look desperately for love from others. Love naturally comes into our lives as we give out our own special light to the world. People who cannot love themselves find it difficult to attract love from others. This might seem unfair, but it is true.

Lack of self-love shows itself on a practical level as an inability or hesitance to receive. And when we are not open to receive, we tend to slip easily into self-pity and martyrdom. Martyrdom may stem from a belief that suffering and struggle will reap rewards - along with the belief that we don't deserve happiness. We may say things such as:

- Don't worry about me; you go and have fun.
- I couldn't possibly accept that from you.
- I don't need any help.
- I always make a mess of things.
- Nobody loves me.

An interesting thing about these attitudes is that they are not at all lovable. Everyone needs to express love and generosity. Having love and caring actions thrown back in your face can be very hurtful. It is important to learn to receive spontaneously and with a sense of gratitude. Gratitude doesn't mean you have to repay the person in the same way; it means opening your heart to the person with love.

Be open to receive in the following ways:

- Say thank you for compliments and accept gifts graciously.
- Be grateful for the magic moments in everyday life.
- Enjoy hugging someone else.
- Accept help when you are having difficulty.
- Be open to receive guidance from a divine source.
- Accept love when it is given.

True love is a state of being; it involves both giving and receiving with an open heart.

Human life runs its course in the metamorphosis between receiving and giving.
Johann Wolfgang von Goethe (1749 - 1832)

Nurture your inner child

Our ability to love ourselves depends upon our sense of self-worth and self-esteem. This is usually created by our experiences as a child. Most parents, teachers and authority figures do their best to help children become happy and healthy adults. Some of us, however, suffered psychological or physical abuse as a child. And even if we have not suffered actual abuse, we may have received love and approval only if we were good, bright, beautiful, or quiet. This means that, at a deep level, we may feel that we are not good enough. You may think, *if only I worked harder, was more attractive, or did fewer bad things, I would be more lovable.*

But it is not what happened to us as a child that affects us now. What effects us now are the beliefs we created as a result of those experiences. The belief might be that we are not good enough, that we must try harder to be a better person, or that we can't be successful no matter what we do. It is our beliefs that affect us now. And these beliefs can be changed.

It is useful to understand how painful childhood experiences have affected us, but it is not useful to keep reliving these experiences and reinforcing the effect they had on our lives. Instead, we need to replace these experiences with new sensory inputs and a new set of beliefs. The only reality that exists right now is what you believe about yourself and how you view the world around you. And the good news is that this can be easily changed. The past need not have an effect on your life now. By using your imagination, you can create an alternative experience for your inner child by acting out a new and different scenario. The mind cannot distinguish actual experiences from experiences that you imagine. Currently, your inner child is made up of a set of feelings and beliefs; these were formed by what you experienced as a child. Some of these experiences you may remember, but many of the more hurtful experiences will be locked away in your unconscious mind. Fortunately, you can choose to change these experiences by imagining and playing out new experiences for your inner child. All you need to do is establish a close relationship with your inner child and give him or her unconditional love and affection. Here is one way of contacting and establishing a close relationship with your inner child:

Exercise 5: Nurture your inner child

Find a picture that you like of yourself when you were between the ages of five and ten. Place this picture so you can see it every day, preferably somewhere special. You may want to put it in a special frame.

When you chance to see this picture, say hello out loud to the child in the picture as if it were your child. Tell her (or him) how much you love her and how wonderful she is. Let her know you will look after her, and that you want her to be happy. Encourage her to be herself. Tell her she is good at what she does. Use language that a child would understand. Always be gentle, loving, and understanding. Make sure she knows you love her and accept her exactly as she is. She is wonderful and perfect just as she is.

Listen to anything your child wants to say and establish a loving relationship with her. Reassure her about any changes you are making in your life and that there is no need to be afraid. Talk to her whenever you feel upset or are about to do something difficult. *Tell her that you love her exactly as she is.* She doesn't need to do anything to win your approval or to be loved.

Talk about things that upset her, and encourage her to take small steps to overcome her fears. Reassure her that you are always here to support her, and it doesn't matter if things go wrong. Let your child know that life is fun, that it is okay to make mistakes.

Talk to your inner child whenever you feel frightened, inferior, or shaky.

This exercise may seem silly at first, as if you are talking to yourself. What you are doing is reprogramming the experiences and beliefs you acquired when you were a child.

Eventually, you will be able to carry out this process the moment you experience a negative emotion, without the need for a picture of yourself. It will become second nature for you to have this internal conversation whenever you feel emotionally insecure.

You may even like to take your inner child for a day out! Think about something you would have loved to do as a child. Maybe something that your parents never did, or something your friends did that you wished you could do. Plan this day in advance, and decide to build into the day surprises that will make your child happy. If you have children, these might be the kinds of treats you would give them. But this is for your inner child. Make this day a really special day for her.

Working with your 'inner child' is a good way of creating the love and security that you never had as a child. You can also work with you inner child to reclaim precious things you have lost at later times in your life due to destructive relationships and traumatic experiences. You know that you have lost precious things or qualities in your life when you become envious of other people's lives. When you see something you love and desire in another, it is often something you have lost, given away or had stolen in your own life. It could be joy, innocence, honesty, integrity, courage or love - all of which can be reclaimed within yourself. What we see and feel envious of is a 'mirror' of the things we have lost in our own lives. This 'mirror' of what we have lost teaches us to reclaim those parts of ourselves that we have lost or given away. We can do this by creating these things for our 'inner child'. By doing this, we let go of dependence on others to meet our needs, and we can then form relationships based on freedom and unconditional love.

Verily I say unto you, whosoever shall not receive the kingdom of God as a little child, he shall not enter therein.
Jesus, The Bible (KJV), Mark 10:15

Forgive other people in your life

What is forgiveness? The problem is, when we feel hurt or insulted by someone, we usually find it difficult to continue to love or be nice to that person. We no longer feel able to give that person the emotional attention or love that we gave him or her before. This is a natural reaction, but it doesn't help to improve the relationship or enable you to let go of the negative feelings you have. Any negative feelings you harbour are bound to have a damaging effect on you. Also, they may affect the way you approach other people in a similar situation.

The first thing you need to do is make sure the person involved knows that you feel hurt and upset by his or her behaviour. Don't do this by criticising the person; simply tell him or her how you feel. Don't expect an immediate response or apology - although you might think that would be nice. Listen to what the person has to say, but don't get drawn into a slanging match. This approach is important because it gets your feelings out into the open and prevents them from turning into resentment or anger. Once you have done this, you need to try to move on.

If you want to - and if it is appropriate to do so - you may wish to take the next step, which is more difficult; start to *give* to that person again. Don't go overboard; just find some simple ways to show the person that you still care. You may find this to be really difficult. Perhaps you haven't had an apology from the person or you don't like the person. But if you try to reach out to the person, you may be very surprised by his or her reactions.

Many of us find it hard to forgive; this can damage our relationships and upset our internal sense of peace. Forgiveness is an essential part of living life to the full. By forgiving others, we are helping ourselves as much as the people we are forgiving.

Here are some ideas to help you forgive someone who has hurt you:

- Ask yourself why you can't forgive someone. Is what he or she has done or said so terrible, or is it just your sense of pride that is at stake?
- Try to understand why he or she might have behaved this way. This will make it easier for you to forgive the person. Has he

or she been badly hurt in the past? Is he or she tired, sick, or depressed?
- Explain to the person why you feel so upset.
- Separate your attitude towards the behaviour from the person.
- If you can't forgive the person now, accept the person as he or she is. Set boundaries for your relationship and treat the person with respect.

The weak can never forgive. Forgiveness is the attribute of the strong.
Mahatma Gandhi, Indian independence and peace activist (1869 - 1948)

Look after your body

Does this statement seem obvious? Why would anyone not look after his or her body? But the truth is that many people don't take care of their physical body. And as a result, they are neither emotionally or physically able to live their lives to the full.

You need to nurture and look after your body if you want to be happy and fulfilled in your life (and not become a burden to others around you). This doesn't mean becoming vain, selfish, or self-centred. You have a responsibility to look after yourself. Life is an amazing gift, and your body is a vehicle that allows you to express yourself. You wouldn't forget to put petrol in your car or have your car serviced regularly, would you?

A table in Chapter 10 of this book summarises the factors that affect your health. These include spiritual, psychological, emotional, and physical aspects of your life. The spiritual, psychological, and emotional aspects causing disease are considered elsewhere in this book. The following paragraphs deal with taking care of your physical body.

There are four main activities that we need to do in order to maintain our physical well-being: breathing, exercising, eating and drinking, and sleeping. It is easy to take them for granted, but the way we do these things will have a beneficial or damaging effect on our lives.

There are plenty of good books on these subjects, and it would be impossible to summarise or do justice to all the good information that is easily available. However, here are some key points for you to consider:

Breathe well

Breathing is an essential activity for sustaining life. All the cells and organs of the body need a continuous supply of oxygen in order to function effectively. The way we breathe is closely connected to the activity of our mind. When we panic or experience stress we tend to breathe more rapidly; whereas, when we are calm and relaxed, our breathing becomes deeper and slower. As we become more aware of our breathing, we can learn to calm our emotions by breathing more deeply and slowly.

Fast and shallow breathing over a prolonged period is not good for our health and makes it impossible for us to relax. Try to get into the habit of breathing deeply and slowly, allowing your lungs to fill up from the bottom. When you feel stressed, breathe in regularly counting from one to five and then breathe out counting from one to five. Keep doing this until you feel calm.

You can go further, if you wish, by learning how to calm the activity of your mind by paying attention to your breathing during meditation. Meditation will help you become more calm and relaxed and can be beneficial to people suffering from various mental conditions. These conditions include anxiety, depression, and obsessive behaviour. Observing your thoughts and your breathing during meditation enables you to become centred in the present moment. This is discussed in more detail in Chapter 9, under Mindfulness Meditation.

Similar benefits to meditation can be achieved by practising various types of yoga. Yoga can help maintain mental and physical well-being. Yoga helps focus the attention of the mind on breathing, and it increases awareness of the physical body. It relaxes and strengthens the muscles and ligaments, and it has a beneficial effect on the glandular system of the body. These actions help to calm the body, still the mind, and bring awareness into the present moment.

A key point to remember with all these activities is that the quality of the air you are breathing is important. Don't practise meditation or yoga in a stuffy room. Avoid spending long periods of time in a polluted atmosphere and spend as much time as possible outside in the fresh air.

Exercise regularly

Regular exercise is essential in order to maintain a healthy body and mind. Exercise increases the flow of oxygen to various organs and cells of the body, and it strengthens muscles, ligaments, and bones. In particular, it strengthens the heart muscle and tones the whole cardiovascular system.

We all need two types of exercise: regular moderate exercise, and more intense aerobic exercise. You need to build these into your normal lifestyle. The best way to do this is to make sure it is part of the structure of your week. Consider the following suggestions:

- Take regular moderate exercise at least five days per week. This exercise should take at least thirty minutes (preferably sixty minutes per day). This can include housework, walking around the park, walking up and down stairs, dancing, yoga, swimming, or any other form of moderate exercise. Some of your exercise needs to be in the open air.

- Do some more intense aerobic exercise at least three times per week. The key thing is to increase your heart rate for a sustained period of at least thirty minutes. Ideal activities for this include cycling, rowing, swimming, and power walking. Running is effective at increasing the heart rate, but excessive running can damage the joints of the body, especially the knee joints. An easy way for many people to achieve this goal in an urban society is to go to a gym regularly during the week. If you wish, you can monitor your heart rate while you are exercising to ensure you are subjecting the cardiovascular system to the right level of stress. There are various methods for calculating the maximum heart rate you should aim to achieve for the most beneficial aerobic exercise. The two simplest formulae are as follows: target heart rate = 220 minus your age (a widely used, older formula); and target heart rate = 208 minus 0.7x your age (the newer, American College of Cardiology formula). The newer formula provides an estimated higher maximum heart rate for older people. The new and old heart rate curves intersect at age forty.

After a few weeks of good exercise, you will begin to feel more alive. You will find it easier to relax and sleep soundly at night, and you will be able to cope more effectively with stress. Gradually, your resting heart rate will become slower, and you will reduce dramatically your chance of having coronary heart disease or a stroke.

Eat and drink well

- Eat plenty of fruit, nuts, grains, beans, and vegetables. These can provide all the protein, carbohydrates, vitamins, and minerals your body needs (as well as other important nutrients and antioxidants).

- Reduce the amount of meat you eat, or cut it out of your diet altogether. All the nutrients you need may be obtained from a vegetarian diet, and evidence shows that vegetarians are healthier and live longer than meat eaters.
- Stop adding sugar to drinks or meals, and cut back on foods and drinks that contain sugar.
- Stop eating foods that contain high levels of saturated fats, and introduce alternative foods into your diet that are high in polyunsaturated fats - for example, a spread made form sunflower oil or soya beans. Use monosaturated and polyunsaturated oil when cooking and when making salad dressings.
- Eat regularly and in moderation. Try to relax when you eat your food, and chew it thoroughly before swallowing. Enjoy the experience, and don't do other things at the same time (such as watching television). Pay attention when you are eating to the texture and flavour of your food. If you chew your food thoroughly and eat in moderation, you are more likely to maintain your optimum body weight.
- Drink small amounts of water regularly throughout the day. Try drinking green and herbal teas rather than coffee. (The extent to which people can tolerate coffee and high levels of caffeine varies immensely among individuals). Caffeine is a powerful stimulant, and it is very useful if you must stay awake. In general, however, reducing caffeine in your diet will be beneficial.
- Find out about the recommended maximum levels of alcohol consumption for your sex, age, and weight, and make sure you don't exceed those levels. Try not to get into a regular habit of drinking alcohol when you are feeling tired or depressed.

Sleep well

Sleep is essential for both the repair and maintenance of the body. It is also vital for a healthy mind. When we sleep, we process problems, fears, and emotional issues experienced during the day. Our immune system is more active when we go to sleep, and during sleep, our body digests food and eliminates toxins. Ideally, we wake up after a good night's sleep feeling physically and mentally more able to face the challenges of the coming day. The amount of sleep we need varies from person to person, and it depends upon a number of factors such as our age, how much stress we are under, how much fresh air and exercise we get, and many other factors. Here are some tips to help you improve the quality of your sleep:

- Make sure you keep to a regular sleep routine. Two or three nights of good sleep over the weekend can set you up for the week ahead, but if you want to function at your best, you need to get a good night's sleep every night. Go to bed at about the same time and get up at the same time. Have a regular routine for going to bed. This may involve having a small, warm, non-stimulating drink; listening to relaxing music for twenty minutes; reading a novel for twenty minutes; having a warm shower and cleaning your teeth; or anything else that takes your mind off the stresses of the day. It is important that this routine is relaxing for you and becomes almost like a ritual before you go to sleep. You are programming your mind and your body to say, *Now it is time to let go of the worries of the day and have a good night's sleep.*

- Don't take naps during the day, unless you are ill. If you feel tired, get some fresh air and try to do something active. Sleeping during the day is usually a recipe for insomnia at night.

- Make sure that your bedroom is a sacred space that you use only for relaxation and sleep. Do not use your bedroom as an office or for doing your homework. Have beautiful and relaxing pictures and objects in your bedroom, and get rid of any junk. You need to associate this space with peace, love, relaxation, and sleep.

- Make sure your bed is comfortable, in good condition, large enough, and capable of supporting the weight of your body without sagging. It is important that your bed is right for you, and you are not tossing around trying to get comfortable.

- Make sure your bedroom is sufficiently quiet and can be made dark at night. If necessary, get new blinds or curtains that cut out the light.

- Keep your bedroom moderately cool and aerated well. Going to bed in a stuffy room could cause you to be restless and toss around all night. The optimum temperature for sleep for most people is between fourteen and nineteen degrees centigrade for adults, and a few degrees warmer for babies. If your bedroom is too hot, you will be unable to sleep well. Your body temperature needs to drop by one degree in order for you to get a good night's sleep.

- Wait at least three hours after eating a meal before you go to bed. Some people find it helpful to have a small snack or nutritious drink before they go to bed, but generally, eating and drinking will tend to keep you awake.

- Do not drink coffee or caffeinated drinks for at least four hours before you go to sleep. If you are a poor sleeper, it is best to try to eliminate caffeine completely.

- Too much stress in your life can make it difficult to sleep. You need to try to reduce stress to a level that you can cope with in your life, and learn to separate dealing with problems from times when you relax or go to bed. One way of doing this is to set aside time for dealing with the problems in your life. Sit down for thirty minutes - maybe once or twice per week, or fifteen minutes per day, depending on how urgent your problems are. During this time, write down the three things that you are most worried about. Decide on the best thing you can do to resolve each of these problems. If you can't think of what action to take, write down the question, *what is the best thing I can do to resolve this situation?* Then, imagine handing this question over to your unconscious mind (or higher spiritual power) to resolve.

- A good technique to help you sleep well is to lie on your back immediately after you get into bed and relax for a few minutes before you try to go to sleep. Breathe slowly and more deeply than normal, and think of all the good things in your life. If you are worried about anything in particular, say to yourself: *I am giving this problem to my unconscious mind (or higher spiritual power) to resolve while I am asleep.* Tell yourself that having a good night's sleep is the best way you can prepare yourself to face any problems in your life.

- If you can't get to sleep, it is far better to do something to break the pattern of wakefulness. Get up, go to another room, read a book, make yourself a calming drink, or do anything that helps you relax. It is important not to become anxious because you can't sleep. We all have periods in our life when we have broken sleep patterns, and if you don't worry about it, your natural sleeping pattern will return on its own accord. Becoming anxious because you can't sleep is probably the main cause of insomnia. Anxiety over not sleeping creates a vicious circle that it is difficult to break out of.

- Make sure you have sufficient exercise and fresh air during the day (see the previous section). Do not do vigorous exercise during the evening for at least two hours before you go to bed as this will wind you up and make it more difficult for you to sleep.

- Try to ensure you get some exposure to natural light during the day.

- Poor sleep may be caused by your bed partner; whether or not it is better to sleep alone is debatable and depends upon your personal circumstances. Many people enjoy the warmth and security of another person nearby, whereas others get a better night's sleep alone. The important thing is to discuss your sleep with your partner in a gentle and loving way, bearing in mind that this is an important and sensitive issue.

- The amount of sleep you need varies from person to person. Anything between four and ten hours may be considered normal. Most people sleep between seven and nine hours. The quality of your sleep is probably more important than how long you sleep and whether you feel awake and refreshed during the day. If you sleep for five hours but feel sleepy in the afternoon, you probably need more sleep. As you get older, you may find yourself napping in the day and then noticing it's harder to sleep at night. Try to forego these naps to encourage better sleep at night.
- Some herbs and aromatic oils may help you relax, but their effectiveness in dealing with insomnia is limited. Having a cup of warm milk or a soothing cup of camomile tea may improve your sleep.
- If you think you have serious insomnia, you should seek medical advice, particularly if you suffer from snoring, rapid heartbeat, or other physical symptoms. Insomnia can be a symptom of many different illnesses that may need medical intervention - for example, obstructive sleep apnoea, anxiety, or restless leg syndrome.

Take care of your body with steadfast fidelity. The soul must see through these eyes alone, and if they are dim, the whole world is clouded.
Johann Wolfgang Von Goethe

Be strong

I am ending this chapter on a very important aspect of love. True love is never weak; it is always strong:

- Love can endure great suffering.
- Love has unending patience.
- Love exhibits great compassion.
- Love does not tolerate abuse.

37

- Love is not manipulated.
- Love acts to prevent harm to others.

Loving someone does not mean allowing that person to do whatever he or she wants. Condoning someone's abusive or selfish behaviour is not love; it simply encourages them to become a less likeable person. Ultimately, this type of behaviour is not in their interest.

In order to give unconditional love, you must be able to love and protect yourself. This combination of qualities is found in homeopathic remedies made from roses. Not only does a rose give its beautiful scent freely (the essence of its love), but it has thorns with which to protect itself. People who need homeopathic remedies made from roses are often over romantic and allow themselves to be taken advantage of in relationships.

Jesus' life gives us a good example of how to love and be strong at the same time. He had compassion for those who genuinely needed his help, but was unremitting in his condemnation of those who abused their authority, such as the Pharisees. His love for humanity was put to the ultimate test by his willingness to die for what he believed and knew to be true.

Love is patient and kind; love does not envy or boast; it is not arrogant or rude. It does not insist on its own way; it is not irritable or resentful; it does not rejoice at wrongdoing, but rejoices with the truth. Love bears all things, believes all things, hopes all things, endures all things.
The Bible (ESV), 1 Corinthians 13:4-7

Affirmations: create love in your life

- I choose to see beauty around me, and goodness in everyone I meet.
- I welcome people and situations exactly as they are; accepting things as they are is an expression of love and a foundation for change.
- Everything that is happening now is for my greater good. I am learning from this experience, and I am ready to accept any changes I need to make in order to be happy and fulfilled.
- Giving spontaneously creates a doorway for love to come into my life.
- I am ready to receive love with an open heart full of joy and gratitude.
- I love myself exactly as I am.
- I forgive people who upset or hurt me, but I set strong boundaries when necessary, to protect myself, and help others to change in a positive way.
- My body is the temple of my soul. I take care and look after my body so I have the strength and vitality to shine my unique light into the world.
- My love is beautiful and strong like a rose.

CHAPTER 3:

Radiate your own unique light into the world

The second principle of conscious healing and transformation

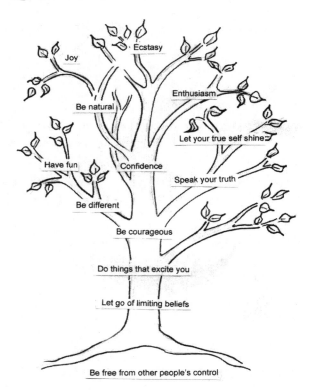

No bird soars too high if he soars with his own wings.
William Blake

This short quotation sums up how wonderful it is to act naturally and to be true to oneself. Each of us has a beautiful and unique personality and purpose in life. You can only be happy and healthy if you are true to yourself. And you can only fulfil your purpose in your life if you are true to yourself. If you are confused about your identity or frightened to be yourself, you will inevitably be unhappy and eventually become ill. Chronic illness is often the result of continuous frustration or denial of our inner desires and needs. We all need to be our natural selves.

Discovering who you are and being yourself is the best way to love yourself and the most important gift you can give to others. When you are being yourself, you radiate your unique energy to the world around you. You are letting the universe and people around you know who you are. Not everyone around you will necessarily want you to be this way. Even friends and family may resist you being this person at first. The important thing is to be true to your inner feelings and inspiration.

Your true self needs to be fully expressed in your thoughts, emotions, and actions. You may be unaware of your true self, or frightened to express your true self because you fear disapproval or ridicule. One sure way of knowing whether you are expressing your true self is to notice the extent to which you feel guilty or angry in your life. These emotions often indicate that you are acting in a way that is contrary to your true identity and suppressing your creative and spontaneous self.

You feel guilt when you do something you think is wrong. This can occur because you have been conditioned to believe something is wrong by people in authority, such as parents. Or it might be that what you have done is contrary to your conscience or standards of behaviour. Either way, the things you feel guilty about tell you a great deal about your true identity.

You may feel angry because you think another person or thing is stopping you from doing what you want to do (or preventing you from being who you want to be). In this case, it is really your lack of confidence and self-belief that prevents you from becoming who you want to be. This type of anger tends to disappear once you stop depending upon others for approval and expecting them to provide you with things you think you need to be happy. You have a right to be happy and to seek happiness in your life, but not to demand it from others.

Alternatively, you may feel angry because other people do not live up to the moral or ethical standards that you believe in. In this case, you need to examine your conscience and decide whether you have any right to impose these standards on other people. If you think you do, you need to transform your anger into positive action to help other people change their attitudes and behaviour. Examples of this might be campaigning to stop experiments on animals or lobbying politicians for stronger environmental legislation.

The guidance in this chapter will help you discover who you really are and how to be that person. It is all about discovering and being who you are, and not trying to be someone your parents, teachers, or society want you to be. The more chaotic your life is at the moment, the more difficult you will find this process. But if you persist, you will begin to unravel the confusion that surrounds your true self. And fortunately, it is impossible to destroy your perfect and unique identity.

Act naturally

Your natural feelings are your connection with the universe, and they tell you who you really are. Consider the following questions:

- What are your forgotten dreams?
- What have you always wanted to do, but have never done?

- What makes you buzz?
- What makes you feel happy?

It may be that you always wanted to go to an all-night rave, go on a trekking holiday in the Himalayas, bathe naked in a cool tarn, or drive a Porsche 211. Or maybe it is as simple as lying in bed for two days in the winter, snuggled up in the warm blankets.

Be ecstatic, not static. Rediscover your natural, wild self. How would *you* go wild if you had no restrictions? What stops you from doing this? Could you do this? What do you need to do to make this happen without feeling guilty or embarrassed?

- See life as an exciting game, not a set of outcomes.
- Be spontaneous.
- Take a risk and join in things even if you are a bit nervous.
- Allow yourself to fail.
- Speak your truth.
- Use your talents to help others.
- Read books and watch films that intrigue you or make you feel happy.
- Be aware of the beauty you see in people and the world around you.
- Wake up in the morning and give thanks for your life.
- Celebrate your good points; don't dwell on any problems you think you have.
- Soften your rules; don't set unachievable targets.
- Dress in a way that expresses how you feel and who you are.
- Be passionate about things you like.
- Remember, you are constantly in the act of creating yourself. In every moment, you are deciding who you are.

Ye are the light of the world. A city that is set on a hill cannot be hid. Neither do men light a candle and put it under a bushel, but on a candlestick; and it giveth light unto all that are in the house.
Jesus, The Bible (KJV), Matthew 5:14-15

Do things that inspire you

Spend some time doing things that inspire you and give you a sense of ecstasy. Build into your life things that you enjoy. Tell yourself; *I deserve to be happy, healthy, and fulfilled.* You are good enough, clever enough, and worthy enough to have the things that make you feel happy and ecstatic. After all, you are a perfect spiritual being made in the image of God.

Exercise 6: Do things that inspire you

Make a list of things that you enjoy and that make you feel ecstatic. The following examples may give you some ideas of the types of things you could do, but you must choose things that make *you* happy. It will help if you try to remember the things that made you happy as a child.

- Go to places that you love.
- Sing and dance.
- Laugh and see the funny side of life.
- Spend some time being at one with nature. Sit quietly by a beautiful waterfall; spend time walking along a beautiful beach with a close friend or someone you love.
- Make time to be with people and animals you love.
- Have a sensual massage once per week.
- Go to a beautiful and romantic restaurant (with or without someone else).

- Plan to do things you really enjoy - going to the cinema or a football match, for example.
- Buy yourself little things just because they appeal to you.
- Spend time listening to music you love.
- Book a holiday doing the things you most enjoy.
- Allow yourself to be childish occasionally.

Try to do one of the things you love every day, and give yourself a special treat at least once per week.

The more difficult you find this exercise, the more you need to do it. Don't let feelings of guilt prevent you from doing what you enjoy. Anything is fine as long as you don't hurt yourself, other beings, or the environment.

This is a powerful exercise that will have a remarkable effect on your life. By doing these things, you are telling your unconscious mind that you deserve to be yourself, to enjoy wonderful and beautiful things in your life. You are opening the door to allow other good things to manifest spontaneously.

Let your life lightly dance on the edges of time like dew on the tip of a leaf.
Rabindranath Tagore, Indian poet (1861-1941)

Live in the moment

Transformation takes place spontaneously in our life once we learn to live in the moment. When we live in the moment and go with the flow, we discover our true, natural self. Most of the time, we are so busy *doing* things that we miss the fun of *being* in the present moment. Constantly moving around is exhausting, and we can end up doing a lot of things we don't really enjoy. We need to slow down and enjoy being alive.

Many of us have forgotten how to live in the present, and we need to make a special effort to regain this beautiful and natural ability. By allowing yourself to be present and act spontaneously, you can discover who you really are.

Exercise 7: Live in the moment

Find a place where you feel at ease, happy, and relaxed. This could be a particular place in your home, a cafe, or a beautiful forest. The place you choose will depend on who you are and what your needs are at this particular time in your life. You may be on your own or surrounded by people. Try not to go somewhere that has strong memories or associations, regardless of whether these are good or bad. Make sure you are not going to this place for a particular purpose; rather, just be there and experience what happens.

Stay for at least an hour and try to remain centred and calm. Notice what is going on around you and allow your mind to drift. Do not try to make things happen, and don't worry if you experience nothing out of the ordinary. The purpose of this exercise is to accept and be happy with whatever the moment brings.

You should practise this exercise at least once per week. Nothing may happen for a while, but if you persevere, you will soon discover how special this time can be. Eventually, you will learn to bring the same state of joy, acceptance, and stillness into other more stressful situations in your life.

In the present moment, there is rarely any genuine stress. It is usually in our minds. Stress develops when we dwell on the past and worry about things that we have done or have not done. Alternatively, we worry about the future - what might happen if such and such occurs. Gill Edwards, in her book 'Pure Bliss', refers to this type of behaviour as giving ourselves a hard time or living in hard time. Gill describes an alternative state of being as living in soft time. This is a state that involves living in the present and letting go of concerns about the past or the future. By doing this, we become more relaxed and efficient. Also, we are more able to appreciate each moment of our lives. It is a state that allows us to be our true selves and trust that the universe will provide for us.

Kindle light in the blessed country ever close at hand.
Hui Ming Ching

Look inside your invisible box

This exercise is fun and will give you some clues as to who you really are. It refers to an invisible box because it will help you discover things about yourself that you may unconsciously hide from yourself and others.

Exercise 8: Look inside your invisible box

Find a box that you can keep handy. Before you throw away papers or magazines, sit down and flip through the pages. Without thinking, cut out pictures that have the greatest emotional impact on you. Include those pictures you like and those that make you feel uncomfortable. Only pick images that evoke strong emotions in you, and then put them all in the box. Don't go out of your way to pick particular papers or magazines, just use those you normally buy or come across. And don't censor your impulses - choose the images you like and those you dislike.

Once you start this exercise, you will be increasingly drawn to images that express your inner desires and fears. Try not to think about this exercise; go with your first impressions and impulses. When you have collected about a hundred images, sit down quietly and lay them out on a table or the floor. Try to group the images together around common themes. It is important that you choose your groupings around themes that are meaningful to you.

Once you have done this, select three images from each grouping that evoke the strongest feelings in you. These images could be those you like or those you dislike. Both sets of images reflect what is important for you and key aspects of your personality.

Now find a large piece of paper or cardboard (preferably a colour that you like). Lay out the images you have selected in whichever pattern appeals to you. You might want to tack the images to the card so that you can put the card on the wall where you can easily see it and reflect on the feelings the pictures evoke in you.

Look at each of the groups of pictures you have selected and ask yourself the following questions for each group:

- Do these pictures reflect things that are in my life?
- Do I want to attract more of these things into my life?
- Do I want to attract fewer of these things into my life?
- Do they relate to areas where I would like to help other people, animals, or the environment?
- Do any of these images make me feel guilty?
- Which of these pictures makes me feel most happy?
- Which of these pictures makes me feel most sad?
- Do any of the pictures make me feel jealous?
- Do any of the pictures make me feel angry?

Everything that catches your attention can tell you about yourself by helping you get into contact with hidden emotions. Things that attract you may tell you more about who you really are than who you *think* you are!

Using the information from this exercise and your memories of experiences you have had since being a child:

Write a first list of:

- Things that make you feel really happy
- Things that give you a buzz
- Things you always look forward to
- Things that energise you
- Work you enjoy doing or enjoyed doing in the past

What do these experiences tell you about who you really are?
What makes you happy?
How much of your life do you spend doing these things?

Write a second list of:

- People you feel envious of
- Times when you feel angry
- Times when you feel suppressed
- Times when you are rebellious, stubborn, or awkward
- Things that upset you
- Things that make you tired or depressed

What do these experiences tell you about who you really are?
What aspects of yourself are you suppressing or are unable to express?

What are you doing in life that makes you tired, irritable, or bad-tempered?

Now write a third list of the following:

- Why aren't doing the things in the first list now?
- What will you do to increase your time doing things in the first list?
- What could you do to reduce the feelings in the second list?
- How will you bring about these changes?

This exercise may bring up passions or dreams that you have suppressed in your life. These passions and dreams give you a good indication of your true identity. You can only be true to yourself, and act naturally, when you are acting in accordance with your true identity. Each person has a unique identity that he or she needs to express in order to be happy and fulfilled and to bring happiness to other beings.

Know Thyself (gnōthi seauton).
Inscribed above the Temple of Apollo at Delphi, site of the ancient Oracle

Stop seeking other people's approval

You cannot be yourself if you are always seeking other people's approval. But it is important to realise that any steps in the direction of self-approval and independence from the opinions of others are movements away from their control. As a result, such healthy moves often get labelled selfish and uncaring. That is an effort to keep you dependent on other people's approval.

Here are some ideas that will help you to stop seeking approval from others:

- Develop your set of values and beliefs, but accept that it is normal for your beliefs and values to change as you progress through life.
- Always try to be your natural self; don't try to compete with others.
- Decide for yourself what you want to do. Listen to other people's views, but make your own decisions.
- Practise saying what you think, even if it means disagreeing with others. Accept that others have the right to hold their own opinions.
- Don't allow people to manipulate you, but be willing to consider their points of view.
- See other people's disapproval as an opportunity to establish your independence.
- Recognise that people will respect you more if you stick to your convictions.
- Accept that some people may not approve of you and that that is okay. If you seek to make everyone happy, you will never be yourself.
- Don't argue or try to convince people of the rightness of the choices you make.
- Value your opinion as highly as those of others.
- Don't apologise when you aren't sorry.
- Stop seeking approval or permission to do things; simply state what you are going to do.
- Try to follow a career that is in line with your beliefs and values, even if your friends and family don't approve of it.
- Trust yourself when buying clothes and other personal items.
- Thank people for giving you information that will be helpful for your growth.

- Actively seek disapproval in small ways to strengthen your ability to be yourself.

Examine your behaviour carefully to ensure that you are giving other people approval to be themselves. The more you support and approve of others' behaviour, the easier you will find it to support and approve your own.

Open yourself to the Tao, then trust your natural responses: and everything will fall into place.
The Tao Te Ching, translated by Stephen Mitchell

Let go of shame and guilt

It is important to process any feelings of shame and guilt that you have. The only legitimate reason for feeling ashamed or guilty is if you have hurt someone or needlessly damaged the environment. The more deliberately you have done this, the more reason you have to feel guilty (and the more important it is that you do your best to make amends).

These are some ways of letting go of shame and guilt, depending upon the circumstances:

- If it is appropriate, apologise to the person or take action to redress what you did. Often, when people have been seriously hurt either physically or emotionally, simply knowing a person is genuinely sorry can allow them to let go of their negative feelings and move on.
- If you can't make amends directly, make an anonymous donation to a relevant charity or help someone in similar circumstances as the person you hurt.

- Sit quietly and imagine that you are being kind and loving to the person you hurt. Visualise the person being happy and surrounded by love.
- Be gentle with yourself. Talk to your inner child and say that the important thing is learning from this experience and acting differently in the future.
- If you feel guilty or responsible for your carbon footprint, decide what action you can take to reduce it. For example, insulate your house, go on fewer long-distance holidays, join a group that plants trees, or contribute to schemes to reduce carbon emissions worldwide.
- When you have done everything you can to amend for your actions, let them go by putting them behind you. Whatever you did, it is now in the past. Feeling guilty will not change the past, nor will it make you a better person.

If you feel guilty or ashamed about things you do that don't entail hurting someone or damaging the environment, it is important to ask yourself why you feel guilty. If it is something you really enjoy doing, is there really any reason why you should feel ashamed? Is it because you were told not to do this action as a child? Were you made to feel that you shouldn't or mustn't be lazy, noisy, untidy, or happy? Are you really feeling guilty, or are you afraid other people will not accept your behaviour?

Here are some ideas for letting go of this type of groundless shame and guilt:

- Talk to your inner child and reassure her or him that it is perfectly all right for her or him to enjoy doing these things. If it makes your inner child happy, you are happy. Talk to her or him as if you were a loving parent whose only concern was her or his happiness.

- Ask yourself whether you are holding on to a sense of guilt or allowing others to make you feel guilty because you are frightened to be yourself and move outside your comfort zone.
- Imagine yourself doing these things and feeling happy. See yourself celebrating the fact that you are being yourself.
- Accept things about yourself that are part of your natural personality that others may dislike.
- Be prepared to reconsider your value system and resolve to live up to a code of ethics that is self-determined. Assess the real consequences of your behaviour and decide whether the consequences of your actions are pleasing and productive for you.
- Teach those in your life who attempt to manipulate you that you are perfectly capable of handling their disappointment and you do not feel guilty. Remember that people who want to control you will often try to use guilt as a taming device.
- Occasionally, do things you know are bound to result in feelings of guilt. For example, take a week to be alone if you have always wanted to - despite the guilt-engendering protestations of your family.

Use feelings of guilt to understand yourself better and to guide your future behaviour: then put your guilt behind you.

Repentant tears wash out the stain of guilt.
Saint Augustine

Let go of suppressed anger

It is impossible to be yourself while you are harbouring deep-rooted or suppressed anger. These emotions will affect the way you treat everyone around you and can have very damaging effects on your emotional and physical health.

I will discuss how to deal with anger when it arises in the moment in Chapter 7, but I am concerned here with anger that has been suppressed from early childhood experiences or abusive relationships in your developing years.

Suppressed anger is held as tension within the muscles of the body, and it causes imbalances in the energy meridians of the body. It can lead to chronic illness and serious emotional and psychological problems. If you suffered a lot of abuse in childhood or in early relationships, you may need to address these issues before you can be fully yourself. Ask yourself the following questions:

- Do I think my behaviour is still being affected by these early experiences?
- Do I lack confidence and self-esteem?
- Do I tend to overreact to certain situations and suddenly get angry or very upset when people behave in a particular way?
- Do I lose my temper more often than I would like? Does my temper affect the lives of other people?
- Am I suffering chronic illness that could be related to suppressed anger? Usually, such illnesses will be of a self-destructive nature, such as cancer and addictions.

If you feel you are suffering from suppressed anger or uncontrollable bouts of anger, I strongly recommend that you contact a professionally trained therapist to help you release these emotions. You will probably find it difficult to release these deeply buried emotions without professional help. I recommend the following therapies, which are explained in Chapter 9:

- Cognitive behavioural therapy that may be combined with an anger management programme
- Homeopathy
- Emotional freedom technique
- Mindfulness meditation

Holding on to anger is like grasping a hot coal with the intent of throwing it at someone else; you are the one who gets burned.
Buddha

Don't let people control you

Gently walk away from people who are trying to control you. Don't allow yourself to be dragged into their theatrical dramas. People will only continue to use these methods as long as they work. The following list highlights some of the most common strategies used by people to control others. Often, people resort to these strategies because they were effective at some point in their lives, or they have seen others using them:

- Throwing tantrums, screaming, or violent anger
- Threatening that they will leave you or commit suicide
- Telling you they have sacrificed everything for you
- Withdrawing affection until you admit you're guilty
- Saying, *You don't love me!*
- Using the silent, sulking routine

Politicians or businesses may also try and control or manipulate us in a slightly different way: by doing so they hope to gain our support or persuade us to buy their products/services. We are all subjected to these techniques in a consumer society:

- Advertising that plays on your unmet needs and addictions
- Cold calling over the telephone by persuasive or persistent salesmen
- Face to face promotion of products in supermarkets and on the walkway

Generally this type of salesmanship will play on some aspect of our emotions. For example: our fears, our desires or our sympathy for other people. The key to dealing with this sort of situation is to be aware of what is happening, and to make sure that you are the one who is in control. Decide if you are not interested and say no. Don't be pushed into explaining why you are not interested, as this will inevitably lead into a prolonged discussion aimed at making you change your mind! If you are interested, do not be pushed into making a hasty decision. You can often get more information on the Internet and make a better-informed judgment in your own time.

The more you practise saying no, walking away from manipulative people, and trusting in your own judgment, the more you will be in control of your life. If someone asks you to do something and it makes your heart sink, say *no* (unless it is a duty you *must* perform).

Don't let others regiment your life and enslave you emotionally. Be the soldier and liberate your emotions; only you hold the power to make this life beautiful and full of adventure, and no one else.
Unknown

Let go of limiting beliefs

Your beliefs about yourself are closely connected to your ego. Your ego is created by inherited traits, cultural influences, and experiences in this lifetime (especially your early childhood). It is impossible to be yourself and act naturally while your actions are dictated by your ego.

Exercise 9: Let go of limiting beliefs

Make a list of your fundamental beliefs:

- What do you think would make you happy?
- What do you think is most important in your life?

- Do you have any spiritual or religious beliefs?
- Do you think you are a lovable person?
- Do you think you are an attractive person?
- What do you think your strengths and weaknesses are?
- What do you most like and dislike about yourself?
- How do you feel about your work and daily routine.
- What phrases do you tend to use to describe yourself? For example, *I'm no good at that. I have a bad memory. I'm arrogant. I'm always feeling ill. I'm easily upset.*
- What rules or absolute standards do you set for yourself?
- What rules or absolute standards do you set for other people?

Ask yourself, *Do these beliefs truly reflect who I am and who I want to be?* Ask yourself the questions, *Who am I? Who do I choose to be?*

Decide which of these beliefs will help you to become a happy and fulfilled person and bring happiness to other living beings. Make a list of the beliefs that are preventing you from becoming this person, and decide that you will make a conscious effort to let go of these beliefs.

Notice every time you think a negative thought, say something negative about yourself, or are frightened to do something you want to do. Try to identify the beliefs you hold that lead you to certain thoughts, words, or actions. Always remember that you can choose to change your beliefs - they are only patterns of thoughts that you have about yourself and the universe.

Our highest truths are but half-truths; think not to settle down for ever in any truth.
Make use of it as a tent in which to pass a summer's night, but build no house of it, or it will be your tomb. When you first have an inkling of its

insufficiency and begin to descry a dim counter truth looming up beyond, then weep not, but give thanks: it is the Lord's voice whispering, "Take up thy bed and walk."
Arthur James Balfour

Let go of attachments

Excessive attachment to things in your life can make it difficult to act naturally and be your true self. We all need people and material things in our lives. This does not, in itself, present a problem. The problem comes when we cannot be happy or survive without these people or things. Attachment applies not only to material possessions, but to emotions, beliefs, and relationships. These attachments are closely associated with the ego.

As long as the ego dictates your life, you will never be happy. The ego is always looking for ways to make itself more important, or better than others. This often manifests itself in terms of power over other people and the accumulation of wealth. Virtually all the problems that humans have created on this earth are a direct result of our inability to control our egos. Here are some tips on how to lessen the ego and let go of attachments:

- Don't let your fears stop you from doing what you feel in your heart is the right thing to do.
- Practise putting yourself in other people's shoes.
- Avoid thinking that you are always right and other people are always wrong. Accept that other people often have different views or perceptions that may be equally valid.
- Learn to accept losses in your life; these are the times when the ego collapses and your true consciousness can emerge.
- Laugh at yourself when you notice you are getting too big for your boots.

- Be aware of how clever the ego can be at reinventing itself. For example, renunciation of possessions will not automatically free you from your ego. The ego will attempt to ensure its survival by finding something else to identify with, such as a belief that you are more spiritually evolved than other people.
- Don't struggle to let go of your attachments. Attachments drop away by themselves when you no longer seek to find yourself in them, and you pay less attention to them.
- Don't complain about things. Complaining is one of the ego's favourite strategies for strengthening itself.
- Do not overreact to others' behaviour. Non-reaction to the ego of others is an effective way of going beyond ego in yourself and helping to dissolve the collective ego.
- Recognise the impermanence of material things in your life and focus on spiritual values.

Become your real self, as ahamkara (the ego) passes away.
Jesus, The Gospel of Thomas (translated by Hugh McGregor Ross), Logion 42

Affirmations: radiate your own unique light into the world

- I am open and honest and radiate my own special light into the world.
- I enjoy doing things that give me a buzz.
- I am spontaneous and full of energy.
- I love discovering new things about myself.
- I decide for myself what I do and don't do: I listen to other people's opinions but form my own views about things.
- I learn from my mistakes and forgive myself for things I do wrong.

- I transform my anger into positive action.
- I do not try to control other people, and I do not allow others to control me.
- I change my beliefs when they are no longer helpful.
- I let go of attachments when I need to move on.

....

CHAPTER 4

Find peace within yourself

The third principle of conscious healing and transformation

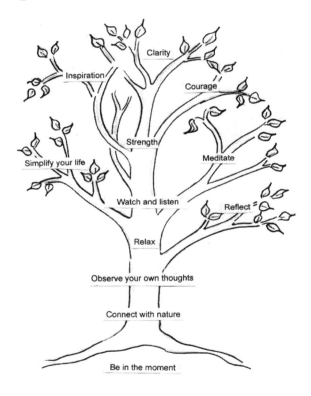

When the soul contemplates in herself and by herself then she passes into another world; the region of purity and eternity, and immortality, and unchangeableness, which are her kindred, and with them she ever lives ...
Plato, Phaedo, 79

Stillness is an active state of being that can pervade your life. It is not simply stopping and doing nothing. When you are still, you are totally conscious in the present moment and connected to the universe around you. This opens up a gateway to inspiration and clarity.

Only by being still can you calm the ceaseless activity of the mind and become clear about the meaning and purpose of your life. You learn how to observe where you are and how to exercise choices about your future actions.

Stillness can be cultivated even in the middle of everyday activity. It is useful to learn to be still at critical or decisive moments in your life. By doing this, you can gain access to the core of your being and the unconscious wisdom that exists within you. In stillness, you can witness or listen to what is happening both within you and in your outer world. What you experience in the physical world is a reflection, or mirror image, of your changing beliefs and desires.

Stillness will help you do the following things:

- Connect with your spiritual being and divine inspiration.
- Become aware of the continuous activity of your thoughts.
- Become more detached from the activity of your thoughts.
- Experience fully the emotions you are feeling.
- Know what action you need to take in any situation.
- Decide what changes you would like to make in your life.

You can only achieve stillness when you are completely in the present moment. To do this, you need to let go of any thoughts about the past or the future. When you are totally in the present moment, it is not possible to experience negative thoughts and feelings such as regret, feelings of failure, or anxiety about the future. You can move towards this state by practising the exercises in this chapter. If you wish to go further you can learn to practise meditation. This will bring you added peace and more awareness of your connection to higher consciousness. The art of meditation is covered in Chapter 9 of this book.

Relax

A good place to start the process of being still is to learn how to relax. Apart from helping you to be still, relaxation is an important ingredient of good health. There is strong evidence that many diseases are triggered or aggravated by stress. And remember, the word *disease* literally means *lack of ease*. Also, if you can't relax, you will have difficulty going to sleep - and any sleep you get will not be refreshing. So it's really important that you learn how to relax and let go of the stresses in your life.

For many people this is not easy. The first thing to do is to examine your lifestyle to make sure that you:

- Do a reasonable amount of exercise and get some fresh air every day. For example: take a walk around the block at lunchtime or a walk in the park in the evening.
- Let plenty of fresh air into your house, and if possible, have your bedroom window open at night.
- Don't overindulge in stimulants, such as coffee, alcohol, or spicy foods.
- Do something you really enjoy at least three times per week.
- Have some sort of structure to your daily life.
- Learn how to say *no* to people when you can't cope.
- Create enough space in your life to relax.

If you address these issues, you will probably not have any difficulty relaxing. However, if you are suffering from anxiety, depression, or stress you may think about learning the following useful techniques.

Exercise 10: Practise deep breathing

Sit comfortably with your back straight or lie down with your legs slightly apart and your arms relaxed by your side, slightly away from your body. Take a deep breath, allowing your abdomen and then your chest to rise. And then release your breath in the reverse order. Allow your breath to become slower, and pay attention to the air entering and leaving your nostrils. Do this for about five minutes whenever you are feeling particularly stressed.

When the breath wanders the mind also is unsteady. But when the breath is calmed the mind too will be still, and the yogi achieves long life. Therefore, one should learn to control the breath.
Svatmarama, Hatha Yoga Pradipika

Exercise 11: Practise progressive muscular relaxation

This is a well-proven technique for helping one relax. If you have difficulty relaxing, you need to practise this technique at least once or twice per day. The following method will take you about fifteen minutes to carry out. You need to be in a quiet, warm, and relaxing environment - either sitting in a chair or lying down.

Gently close your eyes, and do the deep breathing exercise as explained in the previous exercise. Then, starting with the feet, take a deep inhalation and tense the muscles of the feet strongly for about eight seconds. Then, with a strong exhalation, suddenly relax the muscles. As you relax, softly and gently say to yourself the word *relax* (note that it's important to really feel the tension). Now carry out the same procedure of tensing and relaxing the muscles of the body in the following sequence: calves and lower legs, thighs, upper legs and hip joints, abdomen, chest, arms, hands, shoulders and the neck, jaw and the face.

When you have finished the sequence, sit or lie quietly for two or three minutes and imagine a time when you felt really happy. For example, listening to a beautiful piece of music, being in a special place with someone you love, dancing, or watching your favourite film.

Exercise 12: Anchor a state of relaxation

When you feel really relaxed - either after you have done the above exercise, or when you are really enjoying yourself - you can create an *anchor* to capture the way you feel.

An anchor could be a word that resonates for you such as *peace, love,* or *tranquillity.* Or it could be a visual image that conjures up that state: a person, a cat, a colour, etc. It could be smiling and holding your hands together or some other tactile gesture that you can associate with being relaxed. Create this same anchor every time you feel really relaxed and at peace, no matter what you are doing or where you are. This will help to fix this anchor in your unconscious mind.

You can use this anchor whenever you are feeling really stressed at work, or in a challenging situation. Simply breathe slowly and deeply, and at the same time, say, visualise or enact your anchor. This will connect you to the deep feeling of relaxation that you previously anchored in your mind and body. The more you practise using this technique, the more effective it will become. Don't forget to reinforce the anchor every time you are in a happy and relaxed state.

Simplify your life

People who can't relax often have very busy lives. This is not to say that it is bad to be busy, but we all need time to relax and enjoy ourselves. You need to have enough space in your life to enjoy what you are doing (whether it is your work, looking after the children, or other responsibilities). This is not easy when you have a busy life and are constantly under pressure from all directions. The nature of society in which most of us live makes this even harder. Television, the Internet and other mass media bombard us with exotic holidays and consumer products that they try to persuade us we need to be happy. But most of us know in our hearts that these are not the things that make us really happy. The things that make us really happy are simple and usually relate to our relationships and activities we enjoy doing.

You need space to do the things that make you happy and free time to allow things to happen unexpectedly in the moment. You cannot always plan to do things that make you happy, but you can plan to create the space to allow happiness to come into your life. If your life is totally crammed full, you may find that even the things you usually enjoy become drudgery.

Exercise 13: Simplify your life

Ask yourself: *What do I need to do right now to simplify my life? What is most important to me right now? What enthuses me? What aspects of my life are least satisfying now? What do I want to spend less time doing? What things am I doing that are joyless? Do I have enough time in my life to relax? Should I think twice before volunteering for more responsibilities until I have more space in my life? What can I do* now *to change the situation so I can find more time to do things that make me happy?*

Don't try to do too much at once. Start by trying to make one or two changes in how you spend your time. It may mean allowing or asking other people to take responsibility for some of the things you do now. Or it may be that there are things you do now that are not really necessary. Or perhaps you simply need to say *no* more often to people who ask you to do things.

Decide now what you are going to do in order to simplify your life.

Once you start to simplify your life, it is surprising how easy and addictive it becomes! This process of simplifying your life will be much easier once you have a clear vision of who you wish to be, and have decided what action you need to take to achieve your vision. We will cover producing a clear vision and writing an action plan in Chapter 5 and Chapter 7.

Besides the noble art of getting things done, there is the noble art of leaving things undone. The wisdom of life consists in the elimination of non-essentials.
Lin Yutang

Be still

Stillness is the gateway to enlightenment. By practising being still in your life, you can observe the thoughts in your mind and be aware of emotions that come and go. The pattern of your thoughts and emotions will keep changing as you change your habits and transform your life. Your mind will become clearer, and your emotions will become more pleasant. During this process, some negative, unpleasant, or strange thoughts and emotions may surface; do not try to suppress these. *Welcome these thoughts and feelings; they are part of you.* Do not judge or analyse them. They will gradually transform into positive thoughts and emotions as you change your habits and transform your life.

Exercise 14: Practise being still

Find somewhere where you feel secure, comfortable, and can be still without being distracted for about five minutes.

- With your eyes open, pay attention to everything you can see around you. Notice the shapes and the colours of the things around you, especially things you may not have noticed before. Notice any vivid colours or anything that particularly attracts you. Now close your eyes and imagine you can see yourself and your surroundings.
- Feel the presence of other objects and living beings around you. This may be another person or pet sitting next to you. It may be the hills and the trees if you are sitting in the countryside. Be aware of your body. Feel your feet connected to the earth and the air around you. Be aware of your breath moving gently in and out of your nostrils.
- Smell the air around you. Don't worry if you can't sense anything. Simply be aware of any smell that you encounter. If you want to, you can imagine a smell that makes you feel at peace.
- Listen to the sounds. These may be in the room, the sound of your breathing, or sounds outside the room. Try to hear sounds that are far in the distance.
- Now gently say to yourself, *I am at peace with myself and everything around me.*

- Stay with these feelings for a few minutes, and then gently open your eyes. Feel a sense of gratitude and say the words *thank you* out loud.

Once you have learned how to practise this exercise, you can include it into your normal daily routine. Practise it with your eyes open while you are walking, sitting on a bus, or sitting in a meeting. It is about being in the present moment, sensing what is around you, and remaining still and peaceful at the core of your being. Know that you are connected and at one with everything around you. Look for the beauty in everyday objects, sounds, colours, and smells around you. Feel a sense of love and gratitude for all creation. In time, you will be able to practise this exercise in just a few minutes and quickly bring about a great sense of calm and peace.

Be still and know I am God.
The Bible (KJV), Psalm 46:10

Absorb healing energy

Here is a simple meditation that will help you connect to the vital energy that surrounds you. It is useful if you are suffering from any illness or for maintaining your health and vitality.

Exercise 15: Absorb healing energy

Sit or lie down in a comfortable position. Make sure you are warm and not likely to be disturbed for about twenty minutes. Close your eyes and imagine something that makes you feel really happy, something that connects you with a sense of ecstasy. For example, this may be a particular experience, a beautiful place, or a spiritual image of some kind (depending upon your beliefs). *Feel a sense of unconditional love or devotion.*

Imagine the sun is shining brightly overhead. Let the rays of the sun flood through your body, filling you with a sense of warmth and love. Experience how wonderful its radiant light feels. You might like to say the following words to yourself: *a golden sun is smiling down above me.* Let go and surrender to its love and warmth. Now imagine there is a sun shining in your heart centre, and let its light radiate throughout your body. Let it send light, love and healing energy to every cell and organ of your body. Imagine the sun's warmth going to anywhere that you feel tension, or to any area that is experiencing disease. As your focus moves to any diseased area of your body, gently say the following words, *I love and bless you.* Let the sun gradually travel around your body for a few minutes, and then let its focus return to your heart centre. Feel a sense of deep relaxation and gratitude, and know that the divine wisdom within you knows what needs to happen for you to be whole and healthy.

Lay or sit still for about another five minutes, and imagine something that makes you feel really happy. When you are ready, let your attention come back into the world surrounding you and open your eyes gently.

Connect with the natural energy around you. Smell the flowers at various times of year, feel the wind in your hair, listen to the song of birds and feel the sunshine on your face.

And forget not that the earth delights to feel your bare feet and the winds long to play with your hair.
Kahlil Gibran

Trust your inspiration

Inspiration is more than just a random thought that pops up from the unconscious mind. It is accompanied by a feeling of conviction; a deep sense of understanding that is far outside your normal field of comprehension.

Inspiration may come at the following times:

- During or after being silent and experiencing deep inner peace.
- When you are totally spontaneous and acting naturally.
- During a crisis.
- When at one with the beauty of nature.
- When in the presence of a beautiful or enlightened person.
- After asking the divine for inspiration.

As you become more spiritually aware, your life will become increasingly directed by divine inspiration. Anyone, regardless of belief or religious inclination, can experience inspiration. However, inspiration is often described as a religious or spiritual experience. This is because inspiration is clear and absolute, and it seems to go beyond what your mind would normally conceive. Many great scientific discoveries and great musical and artistic compositions come from this level of consciousness.

Chapter 5 will show you how to manifest your intentions in life. It is important that any intention you have is in line with your highest inspiration and benefits not just you, but also other people and the world around you.

No longer let thy breathing only act in concert with the air that surrounds thee, but let thy intelligence also now be in harmony with the intelligence that embraces all things. For the intelligent power is no less diffused in all parts, and pervades all things for him who is willing to draw it to him, than the aerial power for him who is able to respire it.
The Meditations of Marcus Aurelius (Roman Emperor 121 -180 AD)

Chill out

Chilling out is when you relax or amble around aimlessly, simply following the flow, wherever it takes you. Wonderful things can happen when there is space for them to enter your life. Just allow yourself to be 'your self' and to be spontaneous in the moment. Be aware of everything around you, magnifying your senses to see, hear and smell things that are happening at this moment in time - and in this place on the earth. When all your senses are occupied in this way, the mind and the ego become more and more at rest. Then just follow your intuition. Just be still, chat to people or sing or dance. Be who you want to be. You can practise doing this on your own or anywhere where you feel 'at home' and uninhibited.

Exercise 16: Chill out

Try to create chill-out time during every day. You may just sit down and have a cup of tea or go for a short walk. Start by thinking about something that makes you feel happy. Be aware of where you are and allow yourself to be aware of everything that is happening at this moment. Make a conscious decision to let go of anything that you are anxious about, with the knowledge that in stillness the solution to your problem will often come of its own accord. You will be amazed how often the inspiration will spring to mind while you are chilling out. It is a good idea to get into the habit of chilling out even if you have no particular problems in your life.

And occasionally, set aside a whole day just to chill out. Remember how you were as a child, or think of children playing in a playground. Try to get in touch with a childlike sense of timelessness and wonder. Maybe you could go to the seaside, or sit at home all day playing games with your children; maybe you could just chill out on your own, listening to your favourite music. Put aside all the things you normally do, and have a chill-out day.

Chilling out helps you relax and connect with your own spiritual energy. This unblocks channels of energy in your body and allows natural healing to take place. If you do this regularly you will feel better, look better, and your natural beauty will emerge.

Consider the lilies of the field, how they grow; they toil not, neither do they spin: and yet I say unto you, that even Solomon in all his glory was not arrayed like one of these.
Jesus, the Bible (KJV), Matthew 6:28-29

Inhibit your thoughts

This is an exercise developed by Dr Alexander as part of the Alexander Technique, but I am sure others have discovered this useful technique, too. The process involves stopping for a moment at the instant you feel a strong emotion or urge to do or say something. Instead of simply reacting, you stop for just a few seconds and focus on how you feel. You then make a *conscious* decision to act or not act.

Exercise 17: Inhibit your thoughts

This is a useful exercise to incorporate into your daily life:

- Tell yourself to stop at the moment you have a thought, emotion or impulse to do something. Say out loud, or under your breath, in a commanding way: *STOP!*
- Ask yourself: *is this thought useful; do I want to feel this way; do I really want to do this?*

- If you decide that a thought is not useful, say to yourself, *I choose to let this thought go away.*
- If you decide you don't want a particular emotion, say to yourself, *I choose to let go of this emotion.*
- If you decide you don't want to act in this way, just say to yourself, *I could do this, but I choose not to.*

Remember, you can choose to think in the same old way, allow an emotional response to persist, or continue to act on your first impulses. You are free to do so. The difference is, you are making a conscious choice in the present moment, rather than being driven by your unconscious programs that are based on past conditioning.

A key to doing this exercise is to become more mindful of your own thoughts, emotions and habits. As you practise the exercise you may be surprised how often thought patterns and associated emotions repeat themselves in your life. We all have obsessive patterns of thought, emotions and behaviour to varying degrees.

If you use this technique frequently, you will soon find yourself behaving differently and being in much greater control of your life. Use this technique to become aware of and to release the following:

- Strong, damaging emotions or reactions. For example: reacting badly to certain types of people, feeling angry when you are criticised, feeling guilty when you are enjoying yourself.
- Repeating patterns of behaviour. For example: I let him get his own way again, I just want one more beer, I need another cigarette.
- Negative things you keep saying. For example: I am just useless, life is hard, everyone is out for himself or herself.
- Criticism of or prejudice toward other people. For example: she's a whore, he has no feelings, all gypsies are thieves.

We all have negative thoughts and behaviour patterns as a result of past experiences. These thoughts and behaviour patterns are like a strong man that is controlling us. We need to challenge him, and the best time to do this is when these thoughts and emotions occur. We cannot force them to change, but we can decide *not to act on them* (we can bind the hands of the strong man). If you are familiar with the process of Cognitive Behavioural Therapy (CBT), you may notice the similarity with this process.

It is not possible for one to enter the house of the strong man and take it by force unless he binds his hands; then he will plunder his house.
Jesus, The Gospel of Thomas (translated by Hugh McGregor Ross), Logion 35

Learn from experience

Learning is not just about going to school. It is also about learning from your experience and observing how you react to different situations. It is about adjusting your behaviour as a result of these observations and the feedback you receive from other people. By observing your behaviour without judgement or criticism, you can begin to understand what is going on in your subconscious mind. The whole point of learning is to adjust the way you think and behave in order to achieve the outcomes you desire.

Happiness, whether it is physical or emotional, tells you that what is happening is consistent with what you need. However, it is important to be wary of the temporary happiness you may feel when you give way to your inner fears. Giving way to your inner fears can bring about temporary relief, but will often lead to longer-term frustration and unhappiness.

Pain, whether it is physical or emotional, tells you that what is happening is dangerous or not what you think you need. But emotional pain and discomfort can also be a temporary effect of changing your habits and facing the fears that prevent you from becoming your true self. As in the case of happiness, it is essential to distinguish between these underlying causes.

Experiencing happiness and pain is part of a continuous learning process. In terms of learning, failure to achieve something has the same value as success. One should not view failure as a demoralising experience; rather, it should be viewed as an opportunity to learn. The process of learning continues throughout our lives, as the opportunities and challenges we face continue to change. We rarely know what is round the corner, but it is certain that we will be far happier and healthier if we learn to adapt to new circumstances in our lives.

Learning is essentially a process that entails the following things:

- Observing or listening to what is happening, both outside and within ourselves.
- Reflecting on how we dealt with or are dealing with a situation.
- Changing our thoughts or behaviour to try to achieve a more desirable result, now and in the future.

We cannot change the past, but we can change the way we act based upon what we have learned. Learning always takes place in the present moment. You can't learn tomorrow, and you can't learn yesterday. However, what you learn today can help you improve what you do tomorrow.

A particular form of learning is to watch carefully what is happening in the world around you and act appropriately in that moment. This requires a high degree of awareness and an ability to adjust your behaviour in the moment. This type of learning is covered in detail in Chapter 7 under the 'Listen to the Whispers' section. The more aware and awakened you become, the more you will find your life being guided by the immediate feedback you receive from the external world.

Learning is natural process of adjusting our relationship to the environment in order to create desirable outcomes. Learning is essential to life; cells, viruses, bacteria and all life forms survive through adaptation to their environment.

Experience is not what happens to you, it is what you do with what happens to you.
Aldous Huxley

Become aware of your inner world

The world we experience reflects what is going on within us! Nothing happens to us unless it already exists in some form within our emotional body or our thoughts. By closely observing what is happening in our lives, we can understand a great deal about our emotions and our thoughts, especially our subconscious thoughts. Our thoughts and beliefs underlie our emotions, and they create the world as we see it (and the world as it manifests itself to us).

If patterns keep repeating themselves in your life, it is useful to look at your own beliefs, emotions and behaviour. For example:

- If you repeatedly attract people that end up criticising you, ask yourself: *do I have a low sense of self-respect, and am I too dependent on other people's approval?*
- If you keep being hurt, ask yourself: *do I feel very vulnerable a lot of the time, and do I keep putting myself in situations where I am at risk of being hurt?*
- If you don't feel loved, ask yourself: *do I love myself, and am I capable of loving those around me?*

- If your personal life is full of conflict, ask yourself: *am I full of internal conflict; do I accept that other people have a right to be different from me?*

If you want to attract qualities into your life, you must create these qualities within yourself and express them in your everyday life. Be particularly aware of patterns that keep occurring in your life. What does life keep doing to you? Now sit quietly and ask yourself what is going on within your inner world that might be mirrored by these events. If you keep finding yourself a victim of uncontrollable events, ask yourself whether, deep down, you believe you will always be a victim of such events. I think you already (instinctively) know that the more you see yourself as a victim, the more life conspires to make you a victim! Life mirrors back to us the world within us, and once you grasp this reality, you can learn to change your experiences by transforming your inner world.

Gregg Braden, in his book The Divine Matrix, explains how ancient manuscripts describe seven mirrors that reflect back to us our inner world. If you would like a greater understanding of how these mirrors work, I would highly recommend his book.

What is within is also without. What is without is also within.
The Upanishads

Change your inner consciousness

Let us imagine for a moment that the world we experience is a projection of our own consciousness, or perhaps a projection of the consciousness of all living beings. If this is true, there would seem to be little sense in trying to change things externally without changing our internal consciousness. This is in fact what spiritual teachers have been telling us ever since the dawn of humanity; and this is now widely accepted by the greatest scientists of the age:

I regard consciousness as fundamental. I regard matter as derivative from consciousness. We cannot get behind consciousness. Everything that we talk about, everything that we regard as existing, postulates consciousness.
Max Planck (1858 – 1947), founder of quantum theory

The world as we have created it is a process of our thinking. It cannot be changed without changing our thinking.
Albert Einstein (1879 – 1959), founder of special and general relativity

Once you understand and accept this fact, you will realize that there is no need to fight against the physical world. We jointly created the world and together we can change the world. This realization creates a great sense of peace and stillness within us. We have no need to be frightened about external threats or events.

By gently changing our inner consciousness so as to love and cherish other beings and the earth, we can change the world we experience.

You must be the change you wish to see in the world.
M K Gandhi, Indian independence and peace activist (1869 - 1948)

Connect with your soul's purpose

This chapter and the previous two have been about creating love in your life, being true to your natural self and finding peace within yourself. They are about how you choose TO BE. They can be summed up by the phrase I AM. The following four chapters are about what you choose TO DO with your life: they are about manifesting your life's purpose in this life.

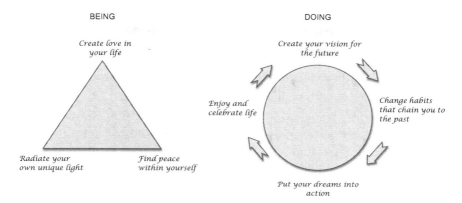

An important connection between being and doing is the soul's purpose or destiny in this life. Many spiritual teachers believe that we choose to incarnate into a particular body at a particular place and time in order to fulfil our soul's purpose in life. Whether this is true of not, there is no question that it is important to have a clear purpose in your life. People without conviction or purpose tend to drift from one thing to another, and rarely find happiness or a sense of fulfilment.

What your purpose is will be unique to you and will usually be made up of number of different elements. Here are some examples:

- Caring for people who are disadvantaged.
- Raising a family.
- Working with groups to improve social conditions in society.
- Developing inner strength and love for yourself and others.
- Working as a natural healer.
- Working in the medical profession.
- Caring for other creatures and protecting their habitats.
- Learning to forgive yourself and others.
- Developing compassion for people and animals.
- Being an actor, musician or artist.

For some people, their primary purpose in life may be to help other people; for some others their primary purpose in this life may be to develop certain personal qualities. My own belief is that we need to do both, as they complement each other: it is by relating to other people that we develop our personal qualities.

If you have followed the guidance given in this and the previous two chapters of this book, you will probably have a good idea of what your soul's purpose is. If not, go back and revisit some of the exercises in Chapter 3 about radiating your own light into the world, and being your natural self. You will need to have some sense of what you want to do in your life before you move on to the next chapter of this book.

If at any time in your life you need more clarity about your purpose and your vision for the future, you might consider going on a retreat or vision quest. This could range from simply spending a couple of weeks alone close to nature, or an organised retreat. Whatever you choose - it should involve:

- Keeping to a very simple diet, with no alcohol or drugs.
- Spending a lot of time alone contemplating nature or in meditation.
- A quiet tranquil setting away from all your normal connections.
- A minimal amount of mental or verbal stimulation.
- Keeping a record of what you experience.

Being close to nature will help to bring you in harmony with your own true nature.

Affirmations: find peace within yourself

- I make time to relax even when I am very busy.
- I improve my life by doing the things I enjoy and by not allowing others to use me.
- I take time out to be still when I need inspiration.
- I contemplate the beauty of nature and absorb the healing energy that surrounds me.
- I trust my own intuition.
- I create time to chill out every now and again.
- I observe my habitual thought patterns and decide whether I wish to change them.
- I welcome both good and bad experiences in my life as opportunities to learn and move forward.
- I am a spiritual being and part of the vast consciousness of the universe.
- I am a wave in an ocean of love.
- I find my true self by being in communion with other people, animals and nature.

CHAPTER 5:

Create your vision for the future

The fourth principle of conscious healing and transformation

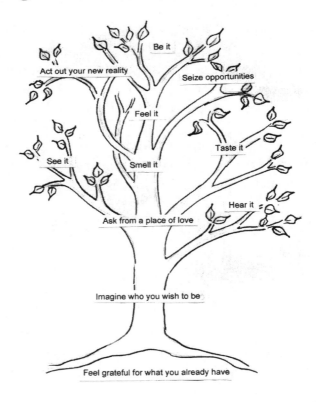

Thou shall decree a thing, and it shall be established unto thee: and the light shall shine upon thy ways.
The Bible (KJV), Job 22: 28

Before you can manifest any change in the physical world, you must imagine things as you wish them to be.

Ask and you will receive is a fundamental truth. But you must ask in a particular way. Most importantly, be sure that what you desire comes from your heart, and that you seek to bring fulfilment, peace, and harmony to others as well as yourself. The exercises in this chapter will show you how to put this powerful principle into practice.

In order to change things at a physical level, you must first sow the seed from which your new reality will grow. The seed is created in your imagination. It needs to contain a clear and unambiguous vision of what you are creating. The essence of what you desire is contained within the seed. The seed contains the blueprint of what *will* manifest itself. Like a decree, it is a statement of what *will* be.

By putting out a decree you are *choosing* to attract to yourself the things you desire in your life. How do you send out this message to the universe? There are some very definite rules you need to follow. You don't simply ask for what you want. When you *ask* for something you want, you are implying that you may or may not receive it. In order to create something, you must imagine it already exists. Follow these principles:

- Be sure that what you are creating is consistent with your higher purpose in life and will make you and other people happy and fulfilled. This is very important. Be careful that what you ask for is not what your ego wants e.g. more things for yourself to make you more important or better than other people. When your ego rules your life, there are two ways of becoming unhappy: *not getting* what you want and *getting* what you want! Happiness comes from using your talents to create a better life for others - and by so doing, creating happiness for yourself. Be successful at manifesting your higher purpose in life for the good of yourself

85

and others; then you will be happy. The only actions or thoughts that do not cause opposing reactions are those that are aimed at the good of all. They are inclusive, not exclusive. They join; they do not separate. Imagine how your vision will bring happiness and fulfilment to others. If you are not sure what your higher purpose in life is, I recommend that you use the prayer in Exercise 29 of this chapter.

- Create a clear vision statement outlining your dreams as if they are happening now. Think, speak, and write about it in the present tense.

- Feel passionate about your vision. Bring it to life and imagine how you feel being this person. Get in touch with your emotions and feelings regarding what you desire. Feel these feelings as intensely as you can, and imagine you are radiating your feelings around you.

- Know that you deserve to be this person. If you think you are not good enough or don't have the right to be this person, you will undermine any of your efforts to change.

- Imagine yourself celebrating your new life, and feel an inner sense of gratitude to the 'holy spirit' for all the wonderful things that are now in your life.

- Include other people in your vision, and create a strong desire that everyone affected by the changes in your life is happy and fulfilled. Believe what is best for you is also best for them and vice versa. Make sure your vision does not involve manipulating other people or limiting anyone else's freedom to make choices. It is useful to affirm that what is coming into being is for the good of everyone affected. Of course, this does not necessarily mean that everyone affected will be happier in the short term.

- Have faith that your vision will come into being. Allow the universe to do it for you. The universe has an infinite reservoir of intelligence and creativity. Be gentle and light. Strenuous effort to maintain your vision defeats the purpose. This is a joyous process full of love and happiness towards yourself and others.

- Be grateful for what you already have and give thanks for what you are about to receive. Bless others in your life that already have what you desire.
- Offer up your vision. Ask (or pray) to be blessed in order to carry out your higher purpose in life.

Write your vision statement

It is useful to write a simple and clear written statement outlining you vision for your life. Imagine yourself five years from now. What would you be doing, who would you be with, and how would you be helping to improve the lives of other people.

Exercise 18: Write your vision statement

Write a simple vision statement in the *present* tense as if what you desire were happening *now*. Keep this statement as brief as possible, but include all the elements that are important to you. Be clear and concise, but be careful not to include anything that may interfere with the freedom of others.

Follow carefully the guidance points given in the previous section, including the following:

- Put yourself in your vision statement.
- Imagine how this vision will benefit you and other people in your life.
- Focus on outcomes, not the means to achieve them.
- Be concise, but include everything that is important.

- Make sure your vision reflects your true self, not just your material needs.

Ask the following questions related to the thing you most desire, as if what you desire has already come into being:

- What am I doing?
- Who am I with?
- Where am I?
- How do I feel?

Use your senses to make it real - what do you hear, smell, touch, and see? Describe a typical situation that sums up what you want to create. You may want to draw a picture or make a collage of what you are creating; or you may wish to write a poem.

Keep your vision statement and any pictures, poems, and other items together in a special place. This could be a folder or a beautiful box. Learn your vision statement so you can repeat it to yourself at random times during the day. As you repeat this statement, it will gradually seem more real. Try to say it out loud at least once a day.

Don't be impatient or get frustrated if your vision doesn't materialise immediately. It will materialise at the right time, as long as you don't begin to doubt the power of the universe. Develop a feeling of unwavering faith and say to yourself, *I know that my vision will manifest at the right time.*

Be aware that your vision may begin to materialise in an unexpected way (and at an unexpected time). If strange things happen, don't run away; instead, embrace the moment. Don't delay, don't second-guess, don't doubt. Think of a car driving through the night: the headlights illuminate the space only a hundred or two hundred feet ahead of you, yet you eventually make it all the way from one town to another. Your vision will unfold as you move forward. Just make sure that you move forward when opportunities arise. Seize the moment and the magic of the universe will unfold.

Where there is no vision the people perish.
The Bible (KJV), Proverb 29:18

Draw your tree of becoming

A tree is a symbol of growth and development in many cultures. It forms a strong connection between heaven and earth, and it can be used as a powerful archetype for manifesting the things you wish to create in your life. Your tree of becoming will have on its branches all the key things you are manifesting in your life. Try and imagine your tree as an expression of the 'holy spirit' working through you. By doing this you will make sure that what manifests for you is for your higher good and the good of all humanity.

Exercise 19: Draw your tree of becoming

You will need a pencil, paper, and a rubber. Don't worry about getting things right; you will have plenty of time to change your tree as your vision of your life unfolds.

Start by working in pencil, and draw a faint outline of a tree. Draw a fairly wide trunk and boughs branching off from the main trunk. Place near the base of your tree the things you need in your life in order to feel grounded and secure. For example, you might include a quiet house, loyal friends, or a stable income.

Write on the trunk of your tree the most important qualities that you want to be part of your life. These are usually general things, such as love, strength, vitality, or happiness.

Write on the boughs and branches of your tree the activities you already do or wish to attract into your life that you think will make you happy and fulfilled. Try to strike a balance between things that involve a lot of effort such as playing sport, and less stressful activities such as walking or singing.

Here, as an example, is my tree of becoming, drawn on 25 September 2012. Originally, I drew the tree and wrote the words in pencil: I have typed out the words here for easy reading. A pencil version is preferable because the lines will carry your personal vibrational energy.

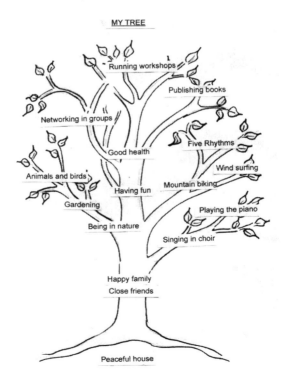

MY TREE

Running workshops

Publishing books

Networking in groups

Five Rhythms

Good health

Wind surfing

Animals and birds

Mountain biking

Having fun

Gardening

Playing the piano

Being in nature

Singing in choir

Happy family

Close friends

Peaceful house

I am the vine, ye are the branches: He that abideth in me, and I in him, the same bringeth forth much fruit: for without me ye can do nothing.
Jesus, The Bible (KJV), John 15:5

Let go of resistance to your vision

Do this exercise as you are lying in bed, just before you go to sleep. It will help you overcome your unconscious fears and resistance to manifesting your vision. Your unconscious fears and lack of belief can sabotage your highest dreams.

Exercise 20: Let go of resistance to your vision

Gently focus on your breathing and relax for a few minutes. Break down your vision statement into particular scenes representing the new reality of your life. If you have kept your vision statement fairly simple, this may entail two to four scenes. Focus on these scenes one at a time and do the following:

- For each scene, imagine yourself in the scene as if it is already a reality.
- Notice any sensations, feelings, or thoughts that you experience. Allow them to exist; observe them carefully.
- Notice how you feel. Is this really what you want? Do you need to change your vision to make it more appealing?
- Welcome both your positive and negative feelings, and acknowledge them as an expression of your inner world.
- Allow the negative feelings and thoughts to float away. Say quietly to yourself, *I am choosing to let you go.*

Repeat this exercise for each scene within your vision. You may discover negative thoughts and feelings popping into your conscious mind. For example:

- I don't deserve this.
- This will never happen.
- This will upset my mum, my partner, etc.
- I can't manage to live on my own.
- I don't have the qualifications I need.
- I don't want to lose what I already have.
- I don't have enough money to do this.

These thoughts and feelings are likely to have been triggered by the scene you are imagining. Focus on each of the negative feelings one at a time, completely accept them as they are, and then allow them to float away.

Say quietly to yourself, *I am choosing to let you go.*
Alternatively, you may wish to say, *this issue will be resolved in the best interest of everyone involved.*

Repeat this process every night until you sense that there is no resistance to what you are trying to create in your life. By carrying out this process, you will progressively let go of all the unconscious programming that is blocking you from manifesting your vision. Unconscious beliefs and emotions are the main reason why people's dreams don't come to fruition.

Our doubts are traitors, and make us lose the good we oft might win, by fearing to attempt.
William Shakespeare, Measure for Measure, Act I, Scene IV

Create a mental movie

This is a very effective form of visualisation. Begin by thinking about the ideas and scenes you developed in the previous exercises.

Exercise 21: Create a mental movie

Imagine yourself sitting in a theatre, watching a film.

- The film on the screen is about you living out your vision.
- Use your imagination to create all the things that make you happy as this vision is played out on the screen.
- You can do or be anything in this film, as long as it does not involve hurting or manipulating other people.
- Don't let feelings of guilt, or doubt, stop you from creating a film of your life exactly as you would like it to be.

After a while, allow yourself to go into the movie and identify completely with the leading actor or actress - *you*. You are now the main character.

- Feel the excitement, the euphoria, and a sense that you are fulfilling your dream.
- Use all your senses to touch, smell, hear, and see what is happening.
- Imagine seeing yourself thanking people around you for their help, and see them celebrating your happiness.
- Allow things to happen spontaneously as you become one with your dream.

Watch this film just before you go to sleep each night (and when you are relaxed). Tell yourself that *this is* your life. When you wake up each morning, imagine as vividly as possible how it feels for your dream to have come true. For a few minutes, allow this to be reality.

When you imagine being a new person, your brain cannot tell the difference between that and reality. This notion has been backed up by research at Harvard Medical School. Their research shows that if you imagine practising piano exercises or watch others playing the piano, it has a similar effect on the brain to regular practice. To your brain, what you imagine *is* reality. And, your brain will set to work developing the skills and physical attributes you need to carry out those activities. This includes developing specific parts of your brain and boosting your confidence.

And all the men and women merely players; they have their exits and their entrances, and one man in his time plays many parts.
William Shakespeare, As You Like It, Act II, Scene VII

Re-dream your day

Exercise 22: Re-dream your day

At the end of the day, before you go to sleep, think through the activities of the day. If any particular events didn't go the way you wanted, recreate those events in your mind in a way that makes you feel happier. By imagining these events, as you would like them to be, you are visualising how you would like similar events to happen in the future.

This exercise will help you let go of negative thoughts and feelings you have experienced during the day. It will also prevent these experiences being programmed permanently in your unconscious mind, where they could effect your future behaviour in a negative way.

Briefly reviewing your day before you go to sleep is a good habit to develop. When you have finished doing this, say to yourself: *I am letting go of the events of the day and allowing higher consciousness to solve any problems I have in my life.* Tell yourself that your higher mind is connected to the infinite wisdom that pervades the universe.

No longer let thy breathing only act in concert with the air that surrounds thee, but let thy intelligence also now be in harmony with the intelligence that embraces all things. For the intelligent power is no less diffused in all parts, and pervades all things for him who is willing to draw it to him, than the aerial power for him who is able to respire it.
The Meditations of Marcus Aurelius (Roman Emperor 121 -180 AD)

Fake it until you make it

You might think you are a certain type of person. However, if you begin to act as if you are a different person living out a different life, it is surprising how soon you will become that person.

The following exercise is a wonderful game to play. It may seem wacky and far-fetched at first, but you will soon find it fun. You will quickly discover that it can change your life. To be successful, you will need courage to act differently and change your usual behaviour.

Exercise 23: Fake it until you make it

Think about your dream movie. How can you *play act* as if it is already a reality? For example you could do the following things:

- Dress differently.
- Go to different places.
- Go on holiday to some exotic place that 'resonates' with you dream.
- Mix with the type of people who might be in your dream.
- Stop doing things that are a poor substitute for what you truly want.

Now begin to play out this new role with enthusiasm. Act it out as if it already is reality. Anything is possible if you have faith, and love yourself enough to try to make it happen.

The magic of this process occurs when it begins to *feel* like reality. This may take quite a time, or it may happen sooner than you think. If you persevere, it *will* happen. All of a sudden, you will discover that the missing pieces in the jigsaw fall into place e.g. the missing person suddenly appears on the scene, or an unexpected opportunity arises. It is inevitable that, if you act in accordance with your dream as if it already exists, your dream will become a reality (and maybe quicker than you expect!).

Assume a virtue if you have it not …
For use almost can change the stamp of nature, and master ev'n the devil or throw him out with wondrous potency.
William Shakespeare, Hamlet Act III, Scene IV

Attract the money you need

You may have included attracting money in your vision statement or on your tree of becoming. That is generally not necessary because you will attract whatever you need to fulfil your vision. If your attention is focused on money, you may be tempted to do things that bring unhappiness to you and others. It is better to think of money and other resources that you need as by-products of the creative process. Money in itself will never make you happy, but you need enough money to fulfil your vision. The universe will take care of this for you. Remember, the creative process outlined in the first chapter of this book:

$$Be \rightarrow Do \rightarrow Have$$

By *being* your true self and *doing* what is consistent with that, you will automatically attract whatever you need to *have,* including money.

The only thing you need to do is stop blocking this process with negative attitudes towards money.

Exercise 24: Attract the money you need

If you have had a problem in the past attracting money, remind yourself regularly of the following:

- Money is a good thing if it is used to create happiness and help other people. It is the attachment to money that is a bad thing. This attachment may become a huge temptation to deviate from love (as Marianne Williamson observes in *A Return to Love).* The challenge is to spiritualise our relationship to money. It is possible to have money and not to be attached to it. Many people who have lots of money are the greatest philanthropists. For example, Seebohm Rowntree, who was a rich industrialist in York, played an important part in establishing the British welfare state; his father established the Rowntree Trust.

- Money will always be available when I need it.
- I have enough money to give small gifts to other people. Giving is a powerful action that brings more money into my life. These gifts may be of very little monetary value, but the act of giving is important.
- I choose to pay people what they deserve for the services they provide. By acknowledging another person's right to make a living, you are acknowledging your right to make a living. What we give, we receive. What we withhold will be withheld from us.
- The universe does not recognise the difference between stealing from a huge corporation and stealing from a little, old lady!
- If I have lots of money, I will use it to help others and carry out my true purpose in life.

Do not become obsessed with money. Discover your purpose in life, use your talents to the full, and care for yourself and others.

Behold the fowls of the air: for they sow not, neither do they reap, nor gather into barns; yet your heavenly father feedeth them.
Jesus, The Bible (KJV), Matthew 6:26

Attract your soul mate

If you are not in a happy and fulfilling personal relationship at the moment, you may have included meeting your soul mate or perfect partner in your vision statement or on your tree of becoming. Attracting a special person into your life is a little like attracting money. Once *you* start to act naturally and be the person you truly are, you will almost certainly meet people you find more interesting, including the perfect partner.

But as with money, many of us have negative thoughts and fears about intimate relationships. These thoughts are often a result of damaging relationships and experiences in childhood and adolescence. The more you focus on these thoughts and fears, the less likely you are to meet the perfect partner. Are you subconsciously avoiding an intimate relationship? Are there advantages or payoffs to staying as you are? For example, you may be avoiding an intimate relationship so as not to face the possibility of abandonment; perhaps you were abandoned as a child, or in a previous relationship. You need to let go of all the negative feelings you have that prevent you from being open to a new and successful relationship.

Exercise 25: Attract your soul mate

Repeat these affirmations before you go to sleep at night:

- I am a beautiful and lovable person.
- I am ready to commit myself to an intimate and loving relationship.
- I am in a beautiful and loving relationship.

Write down the three most important qualities that you want in a partner. After that, commit yourself to developing these qualities in your life. Start doing it immediately. Think about these qualities constantly, and don't allow anything contrary to them into your life. By creating these qualities in yourself, you will attract other people with these qualities into your life.

The most successful relationships are based on love, compassion, freedom, and realistic expectations. Each partner is self-actualised; neither partner needs to be in control of the other person to survive.

When the flower blooms, the bees come uninvited.
Ramakrishna (1836 -1886), Indian mystic

Attract work that you like

Work is such a major part of our lives that it is important to work at something we enjoy. Most work involves a certain amount of stress, but this is usually only a problem if we don't like our work or we don't like the people we are working with.

I am using the term work here to describe something we do on a regular basis that is of benefit to other people. For example: this could be building houses, taking care of an elderly person or designing jet engines. Working involves being part of a society whereby we do things to help one another. We all have a need to use our talents and it is important to make a positive contribution to the society in which we live.

Although there is no scientific answer to what is the perfect work for you, the following are important ingredients:

- Work you enjoy doing
- Work you are good at and that enables you to use your own particular abilities
- Work that provides something of value to other people

I believe that everyone between the ages of about five to ninety needs to work in some way or another in order to be happy and fulfilled. This applies to young children who work at school, adults who need to earn a living, and people who are retired who still need to be part of society (and take care of themselves).

Because many of us need to earn a living, we may have to accept work in the short term that is not what we would ideally choose as a job. If you decide to do this, you should try and be enthusiastic about your work and do it to the best of your ability.

If you are not happy with your work, it is a good idea to include the type of work you want to do on your tree of becoming (Exercise 19). Try to describe the type of work you desire in broad terms rather than as a specific job. For example:

- I am doing an interesting job.
- I love the work I do.
- I like the people I work with
- I earn enough money to lead an enjoyable life.
- I am doing a job that involves caring for others.
- I am working mostly outdoors.
- I am my own boss.

By not being too specific about the job you desire, you open up the opportunity to attract the kind of work that you may not have thought about. This happened to me when I was in my early forties. Although I had led a small team of professional officers, I had never really seen myself as a manager of a large organisation. I knew, however, that I enjoyed working on environmental issues and that I had the ability to motivate people. An opportunity to direct a large environmental organisation materialised at exactly the right time for me. It took quite a lot of courage to seize this opportunity, but it was an opportunity of a lifetime. Not surprisingly, this turned out to be the most satisfying job of my professional career. Since retiring from my paid career, I have been able to create a new working experience for myself using the visualisation processes that I recommend in this book.

With regard to your work, you should aspire to be the best person you can be. You are not in competition with anyone else, but you have a responsibility to use your abilities to create happiness for yourself and other people.

The parable of the talents spoken by Jesus shows how important it is at a spiritual level to use our 'talents' to the best of our ability. In the New Testament, a talent was a value of money, but it is symbolic of the abilities that we inherited from birth.

> For the kingdom of heaven is as a man travelling into a far country, who called his own servants, and delivered unto them his goods. And unto one he gave five talents, to another two, and to another one; to every man according to his several ability; and straightway took his journey.

> Then he that had received the five talents went and traded with the same, and made them other five talents. And likewise he that had received two, he also gained other two. But he that had received one went and digged in the earth, and hid his lord's money.

> After a long time the lord of those servants cometh, and reckoneth with them. And so he that had received five talents came and brought other five talents, saying, Lord, thou deliveredst unto me five talents: behold, I have gained beside them five talents more. His lord said unto him, Well done, thou good and faithful servant: thou hast been faithful over a few things, I will make thee

ruler over many things: enter thou into the joy of thy lord. He also that had received two talents came and said, Lord, thou deliveredst unto me two talents: behold, I have gained two other talents beside them. His lord said unto him, Well done, good and faithful servant; thou hast been faithful over a few things, I will make thee ruler over many things: enter thou into the joy of thy lord. Then he which had received the one talent came and said, Lord, I knew thee that thou art an hard man, reaping where thou hast not sown, and gathering where thou hast not strawed: And I was afraid, and went and hid thy talent in the earth: lo, there thou hast that is thine.

His lord answered and said unto him, Thou wicked and slothful servant, thou knewest that I reap where I sowed not, and gather where I have not strawed: Thou oughtest therefore to have put my money to the exchangers, and then at my coming I should have received mine own with usury. Take therefore the talent from him, and give it unto him which hath ten talents.

For unto every one that hath shall be given, and he shall have abundance: but from him that hath not shall be taken away even that which he hath.
Jesus, the Bible (KJV), Mathew 25:14-30

The most important thing to notice about this parable is the last paragraph: if we don't use our abilities we will lose them. Some of the translation of this parable is a little judgmental in my mind. I would interpret wicked and slothful as simply not accepting the responsibility we have in our life to use the talents that we have.

It is never too late to start investing your talents for the good of others. No matter what age you are, the important thing is how you act today to use what you have to the greatest benefit of those around you. If you see work in this broadest sense, you are more likely to be happy and successful in your life whatever your age and current circumstances.

Wherefore I perceive that there is nothing better, than that a man should rejoice in his own works.
The Bible (KJV), Ecclesiastes 3:22

Heal yourself using the power of your mind

Current scientific evidence leaves little doubt that our thoughts can be used to heal our physical body. The following exercise gives you some ideas of how you can use your mind to heal your body.

Exercise 26: Remove disease from your body

- Imagine an interesting or amusing way you might remove the disease from your body. You need to think of something you can imagine vividly. You could imagine yourself using a laser to burn away diseased cells, or a shoal of pretty fish eating up all the bad bacteria in your bloodstream. You could imagine using a chisel to shave away surplus bone tissue and sanding down the bone with fine sandpaper. You could imagine a mini version of yourself travelling to the diseased area and talking to the diseased tissue, telling it that you love it, and asking it to become whole and healthy. The important thing is to think of a process that you can imagine and feel. Use as many senses as you can - see, hear, and smell what is happening. Make it as real as possible in your mind. Do this visualisation several times a day, including before you go to sleep and immediately after you wake up.

- When you see yourself in a mirror, say out loud something like, My prostate gland is healthy and functioning perfectly; my blood is pure, and all my cells are perfect and healthy; my joints are flexible and enable me to move freely and easily; my heart is strong and pumps blood efficiently around my body. Use words that describe yourself as being totally well. Do not mention the disease or anything that is negative. Fill your mind with the certainty that you are perfectly healthy.

- Be as relaxed as possible when you carry out these exercises. If you introduce something that is interesting, light-hearted or funny into your visualisations, this will help you to relax. You could do the exercise on practising stillness (Chapter 4) before you do your visualisation, or you could imagine something that connects you directly with a sense of deep love. For example, a pet that you love, a picture or place that you adore, or a wonderful person in your life.

- Feel a deep sense of gratitude for the good things in your life and for the healing of your disease. Say, *thank you for making me whole and healthy.* Imagine that this state of perfect health already exists.

- If you are religious or believe in some higher power, ask to be blessed so you can carry out your higher purpose in life. Your wording should reflect your beliefs and passions in life. For example, for someone who cares intensely about animals and the environment, the prayer may read something like this: *bless and heal me (Lord, Allah, Archangel Michael, Great Spirit) so that I may continue to help animals that are suffering and nurture the planet on which we live.*

Be persistent and confident that you will regain your health; repeat this exercise every day until your health has improved. When you think in a positive way your brain produces powerful neuro-chemicals that enter the blood stream and travel to the parts of the body that need healing. These chemicals trigger changes in the cells of specific organs in the body. This knowledge/understanding has emerged from the science of epigenetics.

Our beliefs and our patterns of behaviour are a major cause of our ill health. Perhaps this is what Jesus was referring to when he told those he healed to 'sin no more'.

Afterward Jesus findeth him in the temple, and said unto him, Behold thou art made whole: sin no more, lest a worse thing come unto thee.
The Bible (KJV), John 5:14

Stay young

If you live a natural and healthy life, you will stay young longer - unless you have ingrained beliefs about the ageing process. We don't automatically become more aged as we get older. Science has established that all the cells of the body replace themselves periodically, some on a daily basis, some every few years. This process carries on until we reach a very old age. But the problem is that we are easily conditioned to think that we can do less as we get older; and that certain conditions are the inevitable result of getting old. These beliefs can easily turn into reality, because they affect the way we think and behave. The following exercise gives some useful tips to help keep you young into old age!

Exercise 27: Stay young

• Imagine yourself to be younger than your age.

- Focus on health and youth. You probably have some negative beliefs about ageing, so you will need to challenge these beliefs.
- Don't cover your birthday cake with sixty candles unless you want to summon ageing to you.
- Look after yourself physically. Follow the advice given in Chapter 2 of this book relating to exercise, eating and drinking and how to get a good night's sleep. By doing this, you should be able to keep your weight within your recommended BMI (body mass index).
- Reduce the levels of damaging toxins and free radicals in your body; don't smoke, only take medicinal drugs when necessary, get plenty of fresh air, drink plenty of clean water, and eat fruit and vegetables that help to detoxify the body.
- Involve yourself in activities that keep your mind young and healthy. For example: learning a different language or playing a musical instrument.
- Learn how to relax and have fun in your life; play games, sing and dance, climb trees, laze around in cafes or anything that takes your fancy. Don't let your age stop you being child-like.

Your apparent age (rather than number of years you have been alive) is related to how flexible you are in the way you think, and how you choose to live your life. Once you become fixed in your ideas and thought processes - you begin to age very quickly. Most people who stay young still have a zest for life and are open to new ideas and new experiences.

Anyone who stops learning is old, whether at twenty or eighty. Anyone who keeps learning stays young. The greatest thing in life is to keep your mind young.
Henry Ford

Be positive

We get what we focus on; so focus on your hopes and dreams and all that is good in your life, not what you lack, the problems you face, or what you see as wrong.

- Focus on what is important.
- Assess any situation realistically.
- Let go of past beliefs and dogmas that are not useful.
- Always look for positive alternatives and opportunities in any situation.
- Deal with obstacles and underlying problems.
- Accept that things and people are not perfect.
- Be flexible and willing to change direction.

Exercise 28: Be positive

When you catch yourself thinking in a negative way, ask yourself the following questions:

- What if I could … would it be possible if …
- Why do I think I should or ought to do something.
- Can I look at this situation more creatively.
- Are there any alternative solutions I have not considered.
- Have I exhausted all the possibilities.
- Have I been focusing on the difficulties and not seeing potential opportunities.

Have the courage to overcome your fears and take action.

A word of caution: thinking positively does not mean pretending problems do not exist; thinking positively goes hand in hand with a sense of realism.

Always try to focus on the good aspects of a person's personality. This is especially important in close relationships. Once you start criticising someone, you are on a slippery slope that results in feelings of contempt, the ultimate killer of any relationship. The opposite of contempt is respect. Try to accept and respect other people for their good points. You can view everyone in your life as a teacher. They may be teaching you tolerance, patience, or self-respect. Once you see people in this way, it is surprising how your relationships improve.

Become aware of your negative thoughts, such as the following ones:

> *I think it's impossible to …*
> *I think it's too difficult …*
> *I should …*
> *I ought to …*

You may not be able to feel differently about a situation or be able to solve a problem. The important thing, however, is to get into the habit of thinking in a positive way. You will discover that many good things can come out of a bad situation.

There is nothing either good or bad, but thinking makes it so.
William Shakespeare, Hamlet

Offer up your vision in prayer

To those of you who have faith in God, cosmic consciousness, nature, or any form of divinity, I offer you this prayer for manifesting your true self.

Exercise 29: Offer up your vision in prayer

Say this prayer *once* before you go to sleep at night. It will bring your vision in line with your spiritual self and your purpose on this earth:

Bless me that I may
Fulfil my spiritual purpose on earth
And bring joy and happiness
To other beings and my self

Say this prayer slowly with faith that it will be answered. There is no need to say it more than once at night.

But when ye pray, use not vain repetitions, as the heathen do: for they think that they shall be heard for their much speaking. Be not ye therefore like unto them: for your Father knoweth what things ye have need of before ye ask him.
Jesus, the Bible (KJV), Matthew 6:7–8

Important cautionary note

Do not use the creative process to manifest the desires of your ego to satisfy your selfish needs. Seek out your higher purpose in life that will help you improve the life of people and other living creatures around you. By honouring your spiritual path (God), you will attract everything you need to be happy and fulfilled. Take good heed of the words spoken by Jesus when tempted by Satan to use his spiritual power for his own glorification:

Then Jesus was led up of the Spirit into the wilderness to be tempted of the devil. And when he had fasted forty days and forty nights, he was afterward an hungred. And when the tempter came to him, he said, If thou be the Son of God, command that these stones be made bread. But he answered and said, *It is written, Man shall not live by bread alone, but by every word that proceedeth out of the mouth of God.*

Then the devil taketh him up into the holy city, and setteth him on a pinnacle of the temple, and saith unto him, If thou be the Son of God, cast thyself down: for it is written, He shall give his angels charge concerning thee: and in their hands they shall bear thee up, lest at any time thou dash thy foot against a stone. Jesus said unto him, *It is written again, Thou shalt not tempt the Lord thy God.*

Again, the devil taketh him up into an exceeding high mountain, and showeth him all the kingdoms of the world, and the glory of them; and saith unto him, All these things will I give thee, if thou wilt fall down and worship me. Then saith Jesus unto him, *Get thee hence, Satan: for it is written, Thou shalt worship the Lord thy God and him only shalt thou serve.* Then the devil left him, and behold, angels came and ministered unto him.
The Bible (KJV), Matthew 4:1-11

Affirmations: create your vision for the future

- My Tree of Becoming is sending out branches every day, creating new and exciting opportunities for me to fulfil my spiritual purpose in this life.
- I am willing to let go of any fears and resistance that are preventing me from manifesting my vision and the intentions shown on my Tree of Becoming.
- I am carrying out my true purpose, creating happiness and fulfilment for myself and other people.
- I share my life with a wonderful partner. We are loving and compassionate with one another.
- I let go of any negative beliefs and past experiences relating to money, knowing that I will receive all the help I need when I am following my spiritual purpose in life.
- I use my talents to create a better world for myself and all creatures living on the planet.
- I can heal myself of illness by taking care of my physical and emotional needs, and by sending unconditional love to any part of my body that is diseased.
- Everyone in my life is here for a reason, and every difficult situation I face is an opportunity for me to become a more complete person.
- I will only use my willpower and knowledge for the greater good of humanity and creation.

CHAPTER 6:

Change habits that chain you to the past

The fifth principle of conscious healing and transformation

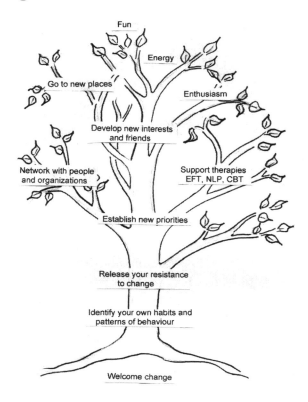

Fun

Energy

Go to new places

Enthusiasm

Develop new interests and friends

Network with people and organizations

Support therapies EFT, NLP, CBT

Establish new priorities

Release your resistance to change

Identify your own habits and patterns of behaviour

Welcome change

We are what we repeatedly do. Excellence, then, is not an act, but a habit.
Aristotle, Greek philosopher (385 - 322 BC)

Once you have a clear vision of *who* you wish to be, you will need to start changing existing beliefs and habits that are preventing you from being that person. Habits are deeply ingrained patterns of behaviour that have become established over many years, often from early childhood. They include your thoughts, emotions (such as anger and low self-esteem), people you are attracted to, and how you spend your time.

The greatest force preventing you from manifesting your dreams is the habits you have developed throughout your life up until now. Habits are like the force of inertia; they keep you going in the same direction, in the same groove that you have always been in. You are addicted to your habits. They make you feel safe and secure. But at the same time, your habits are your greatest enemy because they keep you locked in the same familiar prison.

Habits include the way you think, your typical feelings about people and the world around you, and the way you act. They exist on a psychological, emotional, and physical level. Habits can be useful, or they can prevent you from becoming fulfilled and happy in your life. Our habits can be dramas that we constantly re-enact. Many are learned when we are young, either as a result of our upbringing, our education, or our method of coping with our feelings of insecurity and low self-esteem. Habits that are not helpful include things such as the following:

- Constantly complaining about everything and everybody.
- Not telling the truth about yourself and others.
- Thinking you are more important than anyone else (always seeking attention).
- Thinking you are less important than anyone else (always playing the victim).
- Worrying excessively about what other people think.
- Being too busy to enjoy life.
- Being too busy to help others.

- Staying in unfulfilling relationships.
- Being a control freak who can't admit making mistakes.
- Lying in bed in the morning, feeling depressed and sorry for yourself.
- Being addicted to drugs, alcohol, or cigarettes.

These dramas take over our lives and make it difficult for us to change. We need to change these habits in order to become our true selves and fulfil our unique purpose in life. Nobody is going to change your habits for you. You must do this on your own. It will take courage, persistence, and clarity about what you are trying to achieve.

The easiest way to change old habits is to develop new habits and behaviours. These new habits need to bring you closer to living out your dreams and putting your vision into practice. The exercises in this chapter will help you identify the habits you need to change, and help you replace them with habits that are more consistent with your vision. The following areas are where habits tend to dominate our lives:

- Relationships (how we relate to others)
- Places we go (where we spend our time)
- Work (what we do for a living or how we help others)
- Play (what we do for relaxation)
- Appearance (what we wear, how we choose to look)
- Things we collect or hoard (our property)

When looking at this list, it is easy to see how our lives are controlled by our habits. It is not possible, or even desirable, to suddenly change all of your habits. But you will need to change some of your habits if you are going to successfully transform your life. The aim is for these changes to bring you closer to your dreams and your new identity.

Changing your habits will gradually lead to a change in your identity. It may seem very strange at first, and you may feel you are trying to be someone else. This is exactly what you are trying to do. You are trying to change from the person you have become, as a result of limitations in your life, to the person who fully expresses who you are. This new personality reflects your unique spiritual being and the gifts you have to offer the world and others.

In deciding what habits to change, always remember that you are changing your life so as to bring your behaviour in line with your higher aspirations. Then, your spiritual self can flow into whatever you do. You should try to avoid doing things on a regular basis that you don't enjoy (or that make you feel resentful).

Don't bother to ask yourself why you enjoy or feel passionate about things. As long as they do no harm to yourself or others, you should enjoy them. Be yourself and do things that make you happy. Most of the things we really enjoy do not involve spending a lot of money, but they usually involve time. If we are too busy wanting other things, working too hard, or wasting our time, we will not find the time to enjoy ourselves. This is why we need to change our habits to make time for enjoyment and relaxation.

Through enjoyment, you connect to your creative power in the present moment (instead of living in the past or the future). You don't need to have something or somebody meaningful to come into your life in order to be happy. You are simply happy in the moment. And by enjoying yourself, you often bring enjoyment into the lives of others.

But what about the things you don't enjoy, but you feel you need to do? For example: there may be certain things in your life that need doing but you have never enjoyed. The key thing here is to realise that you don't *have* to do anything. You are choosing to do it, either out of a sense of love or duty, or because the consequences of not doing it are unacceptable to you. In these circumstances, it is best to accept that this is what you are choosing to do, and do it willingly. Examples might include:

- Changing a tyre in the pouring rain.
- Doing your homework.
- Giving a speech at a wedding for the first time.
- Doing work you don't enjoy until you can change your job.
- Visiting a close relative you don't like who is ill.
- Taking instructions from someone who is in a position of authority.
- Taking your dog for a walk when you feel tired.

If you look at these examples carefully, you will see that in each case you do have an alternative; but the alternative is probably less acceptable to you than doing the action itself.

If you can't enjoy doing something, you can at least accept that it is what you are choosing to do. Performing an action in a state of acceptance means you are at peace with yourself while you are doing it. This peace creates a subtle vibration that flows into what you do. You may find that you begin to enjoy what you are doing - and even if that doesn't happen, you are unlikely to suffer the adverse physiological damage that is caused by resentment, irritability, and anger.

What you do on a regular basis - and the attitudes you adopt towards what you do - define who you are. Your attitudes result from the way you chose to react to situations in the past and (some believe) in previous lives. If you want to change your life, you must change *who* you are, and you can only do this if you change your habits. It is your habits that chain you to the past, and unless you are willing to change these, they will chain you in the future.

Your habits are closely associated with what Hindu philosophy calls karma. By repeating the same thoughts and actions, you are bound to repeat the same mistakes and reap similar consequences in your life. Your thoughts and actions are like rivulets (*sanskara*) that run down the side of a mountain and turn into great rivers (*karma*). By changing your habits, you will create different sanskara. By developing habits based upon love and compassion, you will create more positive sanskara and more beneficial karma.

Recognise recurring patterns in your life

It is important to identify habitual patterns that have a damaging effect on your life by destroying your ability to be happy and healthy.

Exercise 30: Recognise recurring patterns in your life

You will need to set aside about an hour, preferably first thing in the morning. You will also need a folder, a notebook, or a computer. Sit down and relax for at least five minutes before you start.

Start by writing down the title: *Patterns in My Life.* Now begin to write a list of the patterns of behaviour that you have developed at various times in your life. Start from when you were a child, and think about how you used to behave then. Much of your behaviour as a child will have been a reaction to what was happening around you, and how you were treated as a child. After you have finished thinking about your childhood, do a similar exercise for when you were a teenager - and then do your adult years. Do not censor anything or stop to think too long about what you are writing.

To give you an idea, here are some examples of some patterns of behaviour (your list will probably be very different):

- As a small child, I would cry when I was left alone in my pram.
- I used to stay awake at night because I didn't want to wake up and have to go to school.
- I used to often be late for school.
- I lacked confidence as a child and never put my hand up in class.
- When I was a teenager, I would go to my bedroom to get away from my mum.
- I would tell lies to my mum so she couldn't interfere in my life.
- It always takes me ages to finish anything.
- I never stick to doing anything properly.
- I always get upset if I am criticised.
- I always get upset when I see my partner upset.

And on a more positive note:

- As a child, I would enjoy going for walks with my dad at the weekend, and looking at flowers in people's gardens.
- When I was about sixteen, I used to like to sit in the local church on my own and feel the sense of peace around me.
- When I was a teenager, I loved going to clubs and pubs with my friends.
- I used to play in a band when I was at college.
- I have always liked playing tennis.
- I like to go to the gym on a regular basis.
- I like to do things with my friends.
- I love to walk in the country.

Once you have finished, put this list away. If you wish, you could speak to your partner, relatives, or friends and ask them what they see as your main good and bad habits. After a while, look at the list again and decide whether you have missed anything that seems important. Decide which of these habits may still be influencing your life. They may be old habits that you have changed, but they could still be having an unconscious effect on your behaviour. For example: I would tell lies to my mum so she couldn't interfere with my life. You may not tell lies to your mother any longer, but you are secretive with your partner. This unconscious behaviour (learned in childhood as a response to your mother's behaviour) may be having a damaging effect on your relationship with your partner in the present.

Now write a list of all those patterns of behaviour (habits) that you think may be damaging your life. For each of these habits, try to identify the beliefs that underlie this behaviour. After that, write a new belief that will make this behaviour unnecessary. Using the example given above, it might look like this:

Learned behaviour   I would tell lies to my mum so she couldn't interfere in my life.

Underlying belief   If I tell the truth, I won't be allowed to do what I want.

New belief   I am free to do whatever I want, tell the truth, and always be myself.

Being truthful is very important. It means you are open about who you are. It is impossible to be yourself and be authentic if you tell lies. There are situations in life, however, when it may be more compassionate to say nothing.

Finally, write a separate list containing all the new beliefs that you want to adopt. Put this list somewhere where you can see it easily. Read this list out loud at least once per week. And most importantly, bring the relevant new beliefs to mind every time you are tempted to do something that contradicts them.

When a belief is ingrained, as a result of childhood experiences or trauma, it may be difficult to change your behaviour simply by saying positive affirmations. Fortunately, there are a number of recently developed techniques that can help you. I can recommend the following techniques:

- Cognitive behavioural therapy
- Emotional freedom technique
- Neuro-linguistic programming
- Mindfulness meditation

You can learn to practise these techniques yourself by attending short courses or you could arrange to see a qualified practitioner. These techniques are explained in Chapter 9 on alternative approaches to healing.

Until you become aware of recurring patterns in your life and their underlying thought structures, you will be unable to stop similar events re-occurring. This is one of the reasons people continue to re-experience abusive relationships, depression, insomnia and all sorts of patterns in their lives. In effect your life is out of your control, until you uproot the unconscious fears and beliefs that support these patterns.

Either in conflict with others or in harmony with them, we go through life like a runaway horse, unable to stop.
Chuang Tzu (c.360 BC - c. 275 BC)

Be aware of the metaphors you use

Metaphors are a particular figure of speech. You might remember learning about these when you were at school! Basically, a metaphor is when you say something *is* something else that is completely different. For example:

All the world's a stage, and all the men and women merely players; they have their exits and their entrances, and one man in his time plays many parts.
William Shakespeare, As You Like It, Act II, Scene VII

Metaphors are particularly powerful patterns of thought that can be easily implanted in our unconscious mind. Other powerful forms of speech include: saying something is like something else, exaggerating things, and making sweeping generalisations. Here are some examples:

- I am a night owl.
- Life is a game of dice.
- Life is a bed of roses.
- My life is like an open book.
- The exam was a breeze.
- It's a new chapter in my life.
- My home is my oasis.
- The world is a total mess.
- He's a rough diamond.

Words have a power of their own, especially when they are associated with visual images. Try and notice what metaphors and other figures of speech you use on a regular basis. One of my clients had the habit of saying *life is hard*. Just think how this might affect her attitude to life and the way she experiences the world around her.

Stop using metaphors that reinforce fear, and replace them with metaphors that reinforce a sense of security and love. Adopt or develop your own metaphors that fit in with your vision of how you wish your life to be. Metaphors create distinctive neural pathways and images in the unconscious mind. They have a powerful effect on how we perceive our world. Use them with great care and awareness.

But the greatest thing by far is to have a command of metaphor. This alone cannot be imparted by another; it is the mark of genius, for to make good metaphors implies an eye for resemblances.
Aristotle, Greek philosopher (385 - 322 BC), Poetics

Plant your new beliefs in your unconscious mind

Deeply ingrained beliefs and the way we express ourselves have big effects on how we experience our lives.

One of my clients was emotionally and physically abused as a child; he is a deeply caring and sensitive person. As a result of his experiences he developed two powerful beliefs that were rooted in his unconscious mind:

- I am not good enough.
- The world is a dangerous place and I always need to be on my guard against external threats.

Both of these beliefs were a rational response to his experiences as a child and a teenager. However, they resulted in emotional and physical symptoms that were causing him great suffering. Before these symptoms could disappear he needed a new set of beliefs along the following lines:

- I love myself just as I am. Everyone is different and I have my own strong and lovable qualities.
- People who are now in my life love me and care about me. I am safe and secure and can allow myself to enjoy life.

It is possible to change your beliefs. The first step is to consciously decide what you want your new beliefs to be. You then need to visualise your beliefs in a powerful way so that they can be planted firmly into your unconscious mind. A good way to do this is to create powerful visual metaphors for each of your new beliefs. Visual images bypass the conscious mind and are relayed directly to the visual cortex. Using the previous case we might use the following visual images:

- I am a strong and peaceful warrior.
- I am an ancient oak tree that is strong and secure.

Use images that are easy for you to visualise - and conjure up the right emotional feelings for you. You might like to draw these images, cut out appropriate pictures from magazines, or download images from the Internet.

It is easier to implant these images into your unconscious mind when you are in a state of relaxation. A therapist can help you do this, by guiding you into a deeper level of relaxation. This process is described in more detail in Chapter 9 under the section on subliminal suggestion.

A picture is worth a thousand words.
USA early twentieth century, widely attributed to Frederick R. Barnard

Let go of damaging thoughts and emotions

It is impossible to feel bad and, at the same time, have good thoughts. If you are feeling bad, it is because you are thinking thoughts that are making you feel bad. Nothing can come into your life unless you summon it through persistent thoughts. You *can* control your thoughts. The unconscious mind is like a servant that can be trained and given clear instructions. Thus, if you want to change your life, you need to learn how to change your habitual thoughts. Most of these thoughts come spontaneously from the unconscious mind (based upon our past experiences and inherited information).

Exercise 31: Let go of damaging thoughts and emotions

You can learn how to still the mind and reprogram your thoughts as follows:

- Sit down in a peaceful place and remain still for a few minutes.
- Be aware of and focus your attention on a negative thought and the emotions attached to it. Welcome them (after all, they are part of you). Pay attention to your thoughts and feelings and intensify them as much as you can. Do this for about two or three minutes.
- Remain still and calm. Observe yourself without becoming too associated with what is going on. Notice any sensations or pains in your body.
- Now say to yourself: *I am releasing this thought and the feelings I have surrounding this thought.* Imagine the thought and associated feelings disappearing over the horizon or floating away in a balloon.
- Say out loud a positive affirmation that counters the negative thought. At the same time, think of pleasant memories, nature, or your favourite music.
- If you feel a resistance to releasing the thought, simply say to yourself: *even though I have these thoughts and feelings, I love and accept myself just the way I am.*
- Sit still for another minute.

Repeat this exercise two or three times a day until the thought and associated feelings subside. This may take a few days. If after that the thought reoccurs, simply repeat the same process. After a while, you will be able to do this exercise quite quickly.

Another technique you can use is to write down your negative thought on a piece of paper. Underneath, write down the individual words of your original sentence in a nonsensical, jumbled sentence. Repeat this nonsensical sentence out loud three times, and then crumple the paper and throw it away.

Whether you think you can or you think you can't either way you are right!
Henry Ford

Face up to your addictions

A long-standing, compulsive behaviour pattern may be called an addiction. Many of our habits are, in fact, addictions. We live in an addictive society, a society that encourages us to look outside ourselves for happiness and fulfilment. Most of us have at least one addictive way of coping with life: work, alcohol, drugs, food, dieting, shopping, television, exercise, or the Internet.

The first step to overcoming addiction is admitting that you have a problem. In the early stages of addiction, most of us deny that there is anything wrong. Consider the following excuses:

- I just love my work. I love being busy. I thrive on work.
- I like being skinny.
- I just enjoy smoking.
- I watch television to relax.
- I don't have a drug problem.
- Having a glass of wine helps me relax.

Bear in mind, also, that addictive behaviour may relate to activities we would usually regard as normal or healthy. For example: excessive exercise, meditation, or shopping.

Once you've admitted you have a problem, try to work out how your addiction serves you. What is the positive payoff? For example, is it a way to do any of these?

- Avoid being on your own.
- Avoid emotions and intimacy.
- Cope with a lifestyle you need to change.
- Shut your ears to higher guidance.
- Punish yourself.
- Comfort or reward yourself.
- Boost your self-esteem.
- Cope with boredom.
- Substitute for real experience.

Try to connect with how you are feeling when you follow your addiction. Ask yourself whether you really want these feelings. If the answer is *yes,* ask yourself whether there is any other way to achieve similar feelings by doing things that are more positive and sustaining. Once you have decided what you could do to meet these needs, you can begin the process of changing your behaviour. It will take courage and perseverance, but once you begin, you will find the process becomes easier and easier.

Even though you have worked out an alternative way of meeting your needs, you will still be drawn to your addiction. This is because it has become habitual and hardwired - not only into your thought patterns, but also into the chemistry of your body. When you stop doing the activity, you suffer mental and physical withdrawal symptoms.

Here is one approach for dealing with times when you are drawn to repeat your addictive behaviour. Stop and take three breaths. And then, for a few minutes, focus all your attention on the compulsive urge. Feel what it is like to indulge your addiction. And then take a few more breaths. After that, you may find that the compulsive urge has lessened... for the time being. Or you may find that it still overpowers you. Don't make it into a problem. Make the addiction part of your awareness practice. As awareness grows, addictive patterns will weaken and eventually dissolve. Remember, however, to catch any thoughts that justify the addictive behaviour. Ask yourself, *who is talking?* You will soon realise that it is the addiction that is talking. By doing this, you will separate your conscious awareness from the addiction, and it is less likely to trick you into doing what it wants.

Addictions can be particularly hard to break, and you should not be afraid to ask for professional help. Some of the therapeutic techniques discussed in Chapter 9 will be helpful in support of orthodox medical treatment and counselling.

Every form of addiction is bad, no matter whether the narcotic be alcohol or morphine or idealism.
Carl Jung, Swiss psychiatrist (1875 – 1961)

Improve your relationships

Relationships are the building blocks of our lives. It is through our relationships that we learn about ourselves and develop our strengths and weaknesses. By improving our relationships, we can improve the quality of our lives and prevent certain people from adversely affecting us.

Exercise 32: Improve your relationships

Think of a personal relationship in your life that you would like to improve or you are not sure about. For each of the statements in the following list, note the statement *a, b,* or *c* that most accurately describes this relationship.

Statement 1:
a. I feel totally free to be myself in this relationship.
b. I feel free to be myself most of the time.
c. I feel constrained and dominated in this relationship.

Statement 2:
a. I never or rarely feel angry with this person.
b. I sometimes feel angry with this person.
c. I often feel angry with this person.

Statement 3:
a. I am never or rarely critical of this person.
b. I am sometimes critical of this person.
c. I am often critical of this person.

Statement 4:
a. I can always rely on this person.
b. I can usually rely on this person.
c. I can't rely on this person.

Statement 5:
a. I spend the right amount of time with this person.
b. I want to spend more time with this person.
c. I want to spend less time with this person.

Statement 6:
a. I share a lot of common interests with this person.
b. I have some interests in common with this person.
c. I have very few or no interests in common with this person.

Now add up the total number of points you have given for the relationship using the following scores:

Statement 1: a = 6; b = 4; c = 0.
Statement 2: a = 3; b = 2; c = 0.
Statement 3: a = 4; b = 2; c = 0.
Statement 4: a = 4; b = 2; c = 0.
Statement 5: a = 6; b = 3; c = 0.
Statement 6: a = 7; b = 4; c = 0.

Your final score will be somewhere between 0 and 30.

If the relationship scores between 0 and 9, you might wish to consider why you are still in the relationship. If you still want the relationship to continue, you will need to work hard on several of the issues (as identified in the next section: relationships scoring between 10 and 19).

If the relationship scores between 10 and 19, you have some serious work to do to improve the relationship. Look at the areas where the relationship has scored low and think carefully about how you can change the way *you* behave in order to improve things. Don't try to change the other person because this usually fails. If you change *your* behaviour, you may be surprised at the results. Here are some clues as to how you might approach particular areas of concern:

- **I feel constrained and dominated.** Decide on something you really want to do and do it with or without the approval of this person. Start with something that is not too difficult. Try not to justify why you want to do this thing, and be open about what you are doing. You may find this extremely difficult to start with, so don't be too hard on yourself if you don't succeed initially. Remember, *you don't need permission to be yourself.*

- **I often feel angry with this person.** Think carefully about what makes you angry. How can *you* change the way *you* behave so *you* feel less angry with this person? We usually feel angry because the other person is not behaving in the way we want them to or how we think they should. Or putting it another way, we want to control their behaviour. But we can't control their behaviour; we can only control our behaviour. So the key to eliminating anger is to change the way we behave.

- **I am often critical of this person.** This is similar to anger. You are trying to make this person how you want them to be. Criticism will not change this person and will probably destroy the relationship. If you want the relationship to succeed, think carefully about how you can change what you are doing so you no longer feel the need to criticise this person. Instead of criticising the person involved, try telling him or her how you feel. Tell him or her if you are upset, lonely, or betrayed. There is an important difference between letting someone know how you feel and criticising him or her. If he or she really isn't interested in how you feel, there is not much hope for the relationship.

- **I can't rely on this person.** This is a serious problem, but it is important to try to understand what has led to this situation. For example, it may be because the person is totally stressed out by work or other responsibilities. Or perhaps, something happened in the person's life, or in your relationship, that causes the person to be unreliable.

You need to talk, make it clear to the other person how you feel, and discuss what you can both do to improve the situation.

- **I want to spend less time with this person.** Ask yourself why. If you really don't enjoy being with this person, you need to be clear about why you are still in the relationship. However, this is not always a bad sign - it may mean that you need more time apart. The danger in this situation is that the other person feels threatened, or undervalued, by your need for more space. Explain how you feel but reassure the person that you value the relationship.

- **We have very few or no interests in common.** This is pretty serious because it is difficult to make a relationship work if you do not have things in common. If you still want or need the relationship to work, you need to think about building up areas of interest that you can share. No relationship can survive on thin air. You need to spend time talking to one another or doing things you both enjoy.

If the relationship scores between 20 and 30, it is working well. But it is still worth trying to improve areas with low scores by using some of the suggestions listed earlier.

There isn't a set recipe for success in relationships. The important thing is to recognise areas where a relationship could improve, be open and honest with the person involved, and be willing to change your behaviour. Be creative and original in your relationships with people, and try to meet their needs as well as your own.

Try to spend more time in relationships that you enjoy and less time in those that seem to drain your energy. You don't have to force yourself to break up a relationship until you feel ready to do so. It will happen naturally, as you develop more self-esteem and form more creative and constructive relationships in your life.

Relationships are very precious; it is through relationships that we learn about others, and more importantly, it is how we learn about ourselves.

The meeting of two personalities is like the contact of two chemical substances: if there is any reaction, both are transformed.
Carl Jung, Swiss psychiatrist (1875 – 1961)

Do small things to show that you care

In personal relationships, small things can mean a lot to people. Small gestures and actions show that you care about someone. It is pointless telling someone that you love him or her if this is not reflected in your day-to-day behaviour. You can improve all types of relationships in your life by doing small things that matter to people. Here are some examples:

- Enjoy doing ordinary things together. For example (if you are living together): doing the weekly shopping together, chopping vegetables together, eating together, and going to bed at the same time.
- Remember the good times you have shared.
- Respect the other person's point of view, even if you feel he or she is wrong. Try to see the funny side of any disagreement.
- Learn to laugh or smile together when things aren't going as well as usual.
- Notice the things that make a particular person happy, and make an effort to do these things. For example, if your partner likes the house to be clean and tidy, make sure you tidy up your things and contribute to cleaning.

- Make a conscious effort not to be critical of people. If someone has upset you, try to tell that person in a non-threatening way.
- Accept that you may have habits that irritate another person, and do your best to deal with these. Don't nag your partner, but tell them when something really irritates you (tactfully, of course).
- Learn how to touch people you care about in a loving and non-sexual way.
- Listen to and be sensitive to other people's emotions and areas of vulnerability. Understand that everyone is vulnerable in different ways.
- Be there, but don't put demands upon people when they are unwell or going through a crisis.
- Create mystery and fun in your relationships. Don't allow your relationships to become boring or mundane.

If you cannot do great things, do small things in a great way.
Napoleon Hill, American author (1883 – 1970)

Welcome new relationships

Although it is important to try to improve your existing relationships, it is equally important to open the doorway to new relationships, particularly those that reflect who you are and the vision you have for your life. You will begin to form new relationships as you change other habits, such as the places you go and the activities you take part in.

Think about what sorts of people you would like in your life. Try to imagine what you would need to do to meet these sorts of people. This may involve going to new places or taking up new interests. But make sure that you are being true to yourself. The best way to attract the right people into your life is to be yourself, no matter where you are. This may take a lot of courage, especially if you are shy around new people.

If you want to improve your relationship within a group, or with a person, pay attention to what is happening and what is being said. Show that you are interested; that you care about the group or the person. Be enthusiastic and honest in terms of what you say and do.

When you meet someone who you are particularly attracted to, make sure you do something to communicate that feeling to him or her. This could entail smiling at an appropriate time, or making it clear in some other way that you are interested in the person. Here are some good tips for developing a relationship with someone:

- Say something. You may not have another opportunity.
- Use the person's name.
- Listen carefully and show the person you are interested in what he or she is saying. Try to discover what he or she likes to do, where he or she likes to go. Talk about things that interest the person.
- Ask him or her about his or her feelings. Be kind and sympathetic.
- Be aware of making eye contact, but don't stare.
- Be generous.
- Make the person feel special. Comment on things you like about him or her.
- Be gentle and persistent (but don't harass the person). Try and act confidently even if you feel nervous.
- Be relaxed and have a sense of humour.
- Be honest about your feelings, but don't moan or look for sympathy.
- If and when it is appropriate, touch him or her in a caring, non-threatening way.
- Once you know the person a little, try to move the conversation towards more personal matters (these are the things that are important to most people).

- If you are getting the wrong vibes from the person, respect his or her space and move on. Nobody likes to be harassed, and it does nothing for your self-respect.

Most of the points listed in this section apply to creating a meaningful relationship with anyone - even people you may not like. Everybody can teach us something about ourselves. We may dislike people who mirror behaviour that we have overcome in ourselves, people that have completely different values, or people who have already got the things we desire. But if you think about it carefully, in every case they can tell us something about ourselves. We tend to attract into our lives the people that mirror what is going on in our unconscious world. Don't reject too easily people who cross your path - they usually have a purpose in your life.

The quickest and easiest way to change your life is to change the people in your life. And remember, when forming a romantic relationship: love feeds on mystery.
The author

Learn how to resolve conflict

Conflict occurs in all walks of life. It can cause the breakdown of relationships and lead to violence and wars. Alternatively, it can open up avenues for change and the development of new relationships and opportunities. How you deal with conflict will have a destructive or constructive effect on your life, and the lives of those around you. There are four possible responses to conflict:

Withdrawal
One natural response to conflict is to run away or withdraw from a situation. We can do this literally when there is a threat to our safety, or we can do this emotionally when we are upset. It can be

useful in extreme situations, but it has a downside: you no longer have a say in what happens, and the problem may continue to grow out of proportion. On the upside: it may prevent you from being hurt, allow time for the situation to subside, or allow time for the other person to calm down. Temporarily withdrawing from a conflict or argument can be the best thing to do when things are getting out of control.

Ignore the conflict

Another response is to refuse to acknowledge the conflict. This can be effective in some situations. By not reacting and ignoring aggressive behaviour, we are not contributing to the conflict, and the other party may calm down. However, in emotional situations, the opposite may be true: the other party may be incensed by the fact that we have not reacted. Turning the other cheek is more likely to be effective if you can do this without harbouring any irritation or anger. If you are suppressing negative emotions, this can be damaging to you, and your emotions will probably erupt at some point in the future. Also, when you are silent, the other person doesn't find out your point of view or know what you are feeling.

Decide to fight

You can decide to confront the conflict head on. There are three likely outcomes: you win, you lose, or you both lose. The possibility that you can both win is unlikely. The problem with this strategy is that, even if you think you have won, you may have destroyed or angered the other party; or they may simply retreat and decide to fight another day. Deciding to fight is usually the worst way to deal with conflict, but it may be necessary in some circumstances to protect yourself or others from harm.

Resolve the conflict

The objective here is to achieve a win/win outcome by thinking creatively and discovering alternative and better solutions to a situation. Two preconditions for resolving conflict are that all parties concerned want to end the conflict, and all parties are prepared to talk to one another. Has one of the parties a reason for maintaining the conflict? Are they gaining more by keeping the conflict alive? Many conflicts on the worldwide stage continue because politicians or powerful businesses have vested interests in maintaining the conflict. Similarly, there may be conscious or subconscious reasons why a person wants to continue a personal dispute with another person. Before progress can be made, these need to be identified and resolved. The next stage in resolving conflict is to identify areas of agreement or common interest. Once this point has been reached, it is usually possible to agree on some form of compromise that will resolve the conflict.

There are times when withdrawal, ignoring a conflict, or deciding to fight are the sensible options; but the best solution to conflict is to seek resolution through mutual understanding and agreement. This will nearly always require negotiation and compromise on the part of the people involved.

When you are in conflict, try not to react in an impulsive way. If possible, try to de-escalate the situation. Think, *What would a wise and compassionate person do in this situation?* There are times when a wise person would ignore conflict or walk away, and there are times when it may be necessary to stand up and fight. But try to develop the habits and skills to resolve conflicts. This is always the best way, and it creates the greatest rewards for all parties.

Man must evolve for all human conflict a method which rejects revenge, aggression and retaliation. The foundation of such a method is love.
Martin Luther King, Jr

Go to new places

Think about your vision of who you want to be. Where would you be if you were truly being yourself? Don't allow yourself to censor your thoughts. Simply allow yourself to dream your highest dream. See yourself being happy and bringing happiness into the lives of others.

Exercise 33: Go to new places

Write a list of places where you like to be or would like to go. Here is my list, but your list will be personal to you:

- By a warm fire at home
- In a beautiful forest
- In a magnificent church or cathedral
- At the Heart Centre in Headingley
- At the Peace Café in Halifax
- In the Lake District
- At Zeffirellis restaurant in Ambleside
- Collioure
- Corsica
- Stratford on Avon
- Prague

Decide on the places you want to go and *go* there. If you find places where you feel a sense of peace and calm, try to go there as often as you can. Notice where you meet people that you seem to like. Stop going to places that make you feel agitated or where you feel out of place. Notice where you feel happy and try and go there more often.

Where would you be able to be yourself and act according to your highest nature? What is stopping you from spending time in these places? If you want to share the experience with another person, what can you do to make this happen? Perhaps you should go to these places on your own, and imagine you are with the kind of person you want to be with. You might go on a walking holiday on your own. You might join a choir or go to Taiwan. Have the courage to go to the places that enthuse you.

If you are trying to meet a partner or new friends, you are most likely to meet these people if you go to places and do things you enjoy. The same qualities will also attract them. If you go to the places you always go to, you will probably meet the same sorts of people you met in the past. One of the keys to success is to expose oneself to new experiences. This usually entails going to new places. After all, places have their own special character and energy.

All species of plants and animals are adapted to different environments. Discover places where you come to life, and create time to be there.
The author

Break the chains that bind you

Breaking habits always involves doing new things and doing fewer of the things you normally do. This means you must be prepared to face your fears and move outside your comfort zone. Try to do things you really enjoy doing, even if this is difficult. Pitch your efforts at a level that you think you can achieve by making a determined effort. Don't try to do things that are impossible for you at the moment, but be prepared to push yourself outside your comfort zone. When possible, focus on things that are consistent with your vision, but don't be frightened to welcome the unknown into your life.

Here are some examples of how you might take more risks in your life and change the habits that bind you to your existing patterns of behaviour:

- Have the courage to follow your heart and act in a way that feels right for you in the moment, even if it is contrary to what you would do normally. Try new things; seize the day!
- Imagine small things you could do to make other people's lives more enjoyable. Commit yourself to doing these things, even though you may feel some fear or apprehension.
- Teach yourself to be brave in small ways. Set yourself small challenges to overcome, to build up your self-confidence, so you can face greater challenges in the future. Break down major tasks into small steps.
- Accept that you are frightened to do something and do it anyway. The more you practise this approach, the easier it will be to overcome your fears.
- Look for support around you. Start identifying friends who have done something similar, or try to meet new people with similar aspirations and goals.
- Identify role models you would like to emulate, and find out as much as you can about their lifestyle, beliefs, and attitudes.
- Accept that you can't make meaningful changes in your life without making mistakes and looking silly at times. But, avoid exposing yourself to very challenging situations before you are ready, and don't beat yourself up if you fail. Try not to think in terms of failure; see everything as an opportunity to learn.
- Welcome new experiences and new people into your life. Be excited about meeting new and different people. Talk to people you have avoided in the past. Try not to judge people by their appearances.
- Do things on impulse. Learn how to be spontaneous. Take risks to escape from routine. Be prepared to fail or look ridiculous.

- Accept that changing your habits will mean a certain amount of personal upheaval. It may mean doing things that you have always avoided.

Don't let convictions and beliefs formed by past experiences keep you immobilised.

Excellence is an art won by training and habituation. We do not act rightly because we have virtue or excellence, but rather have those because we have acted rightly. We are what we repeatedly do. Excellence, then, is not an act but a habit.
Aristotle (384 BC - 322 BC)

Welcome change

Once you start to change your habits and act in accordance with your true self, it is important to become aware of your thoughts and emotional reactions. In some areas, there will be a strong tendency to resist change. You may become temporarily anxious about your new identity. Old fears (or new fears) will emerge, and it is important to deal with these if you want to progress towards your goals. Eventually, you will become more confident that you can change your habits. You will then begin to welcome change in your life. You will realise that a bend in the road is only the end of the road if you fail to change direction!

Failure to move on in your life can lead to depression and other forms of mental illness.

That which does not kill a man makes him stronger
Nietzche

Affirmations: change habits that chain you to the past

- I notice patterns that repeat themselves in my life.
- I use inspiring metaphors to describe myself and my life.
- I change my beliefs to improve my life and the lives of others.
- I let go of damaging thoughts and emotions.
- I let go of addictive behaviour.
- I work constantly to improve the relationship I have with everyone who is in my life.
- I do small acts of kindness to make other people feel happy.
- I am open to form new and different relationships in my life.
- I resolve rather than create conflict in my life.
- I enjoy going to places where I have not been before.
- I let go of unhelpful habits that are linked to my past.
- I am excited and optimistic about changes that are taking place in my life.

CHAPTER 7:

Put your dreams into action

The sixth principle of conscious healing and transformation

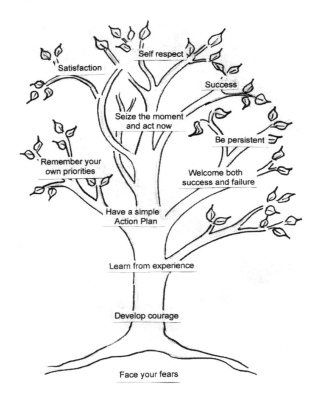

Whatever you can do or dream you can do, begin it. Boldness has genius, power and magic in it.
Goethe

You must start changing right now. It's no good thinking you will start changing tomorrow. You have probably heard the saying: tomorrow never comes. This is true because, when you get to tomorrow, it will be today - and chances are that you will continue to put off doing what you need to do to change your life. The good news is that you don't have to change your whole world in a day. What you must do is start to change a little of your world today.

By acting now, you are giving a clear message to the universe that you are really committed to changing your life. The universe will respond by creating countless opportunities to help you on your path. Your actions don't have to be large or difficult. Small actions will unlock the creative forces of the universe. But you must be persistent and take every small opportunity to act out your vision. It is no good having a wonderful vision if you are not prepared to start making changes in your life now. You don't need to do the impossible! These changes can be small, but it is essential that they are consistent with your true identity and dreams. It is better to take many small steps in the right direction than to attempt to make massive changes that will cause you to panic and lose confidence.

You must find the courage to act. Courage is daring to take the first step on a different path. It is the decision to place your dreams above your fears. Acting *now* means changing your habits as outlined in the previous chapter. It also means responding creatively to the situation you are in right now and seizing any new opportunities that arise during the day. As you get into the habit of responding creatively to new situations, you will be surprised how the opportunities you desire seem to arise spontaneously. The more you live in the moment and act on small opportunities, the more opportunities will miraculously appear in your life. You will also become aware of a strange synchronicity that starts to appear in your life.

Always remember, when opportunities arise, try to put your fears to one side and act in accordance with your higher vision.

In practice, you will need an action plan. Your action plan will include the actions you are going to take in order to bring your vision into reality. It is important that you stick to your plan; but that is not to say that you can never change your action plan. It is okay to change your plan when new opportunities arise, but not because you are avoiding putting your plan into action. You may want to change your plan almost immediately after you start to implement it! This is usually a sign that you are subconsciously frightened of something - perhaps the very fear that has prevented you from making changes in the past. There are techniques (explained later in this chapter) that will help you to let go of the fears that are sabotaging your efforts to change. You need to use these techniques immediately you sense resistance to change, or feel uncertain about what you are doing. It is important to deal with your fears as soon as they arise and not allow them to fester and grow larger. If you run away from your fears, they will become a major stumbling block. Fears are the reason we continue to sabotage our lives. If we are to change, we need to embrace our fears as they occur.

Change requires that we take risks and move out of our comfort zone. As we do this, we will experience various degrees of fear (ranging from a sense of uneasiness to absolute panic). We don't need to overcome these fears immediately, we simply need to be aware of them and release them gradually. The process for doing this is not an aggressive one. You cannot *force* your fears to go away. The process is one of gentle acceptance and letting go. Courage is required to face your fears and continue doing the things you want or need to do. Everyone has experienced the fear of changing things in their lives. For some people, it can be the fear of getting out of bed or changing your job or giving a presentation to a group of colleagues. The things that frighten you depend upon your personality and past experiences. Bad experiences are those that upset you emotionally. What is a bad experience for one person may be a challenge to another. Note that there are three types of fear common to all people, which manifest as specific emotions.

TYPE OF FEAR	EXPRESSED IN THE EMOTIONS OF
Insecurity, fear of being hurt or dying.	Anxiety, panic, paranoia and obsessive thoughts/behaviour.
Being unloved and rejected.	Desperate for love and approval. Obsessive behaviour, sadness and depression.
Unable to express oneself.	Anger, desire to control others, feelings of inadequacy, guilt and depression.

These fears and emotions are the main reasons why people fail to change, even though they may know who they would like to be and what they would like to do. You need to let go of your fears and take a few risks in order to expand your world. Accept that you may feel insecure, panic, or feel embarrassed at first. Don't try to do the impossible, but be prepared to gradually move outside your comfort zone. As you take more risks and discover that you can survive the consequences, your fears will diminish.

Create an action plan

Creating an action plan is about putting in writing your commitment to change. It is about the action that you are determined to take to turn your vision/dreams into reality. It should be like a contract with yourself.

Until there is commitment, there is hesitancy, the chance to draw back, always ineffectiveness. Concerning all acts of initiative (and creation) there is one elementary truth, the ignorance of which kills countless ideas and splendid plans: that the moment one definitely commits oneself then Providence moves too. All sorts of things occur to help one that would never otherwise have occurred. A whole stream of events issues forth from the decision, raising in one's favour all manner of unforeseen incidents

and meetings and material assistance which no man could have dreamed would have come his way. Whatever you can do or dream you can, begin it. Boldness has genius, power and magic in it. Begin it now.
Johann Wolfgang von Goethe

Exercise 34: Create an action plan

Create an action plan that will help you change your habits and manifest the life you desire. But remember, an action plan is of no value if you fail to put it into action! The basis of your plan should be as follows:

- Your vision statement and tree of becoming (see Chapter 5)
- Habits you need to change (see Chapter 6).

If you feel you need to make a lot of changes in your life, you should initially set about seven key intentions. These are goals that you will achieve now or in the next few months. Some of these should relate directly to your vision statement and your tree of becoming, and some should be aimed at changing key habits that are sabotaging your efforts to change. For each intention, you can set as many specific targets as you like. At least half of your targets should be achievable within four weeks. The following is an example of what an action plan might look like.

ACTION PLAN 22 DECEMBER 2011

INTENTION	TARGETS
1 Feel fit and full of energy.	(a) Go to the gym twice a week and do 40 minutes cardiovascular exercise each visit. (b) Join a badminton club this week.
2 Feel calm and relaxed.	(a) Have one quiet evening a week at home on my own. (b) Go to Yoga class once a week starting at beginning of January.
3 Share my time with interesting people.	(a) Go to one new class, group or activity every month until I meet a group of people I enjoy being with. (b) Book a group activity holiday in January for this summer.
4 Spend less time with people and/or in situations that make me feel unhappy.	(a) Say no to people when I don't want to do something and don't explain why. (b) Be positive and don't be provoked into arguments.
5 Be in a job I really enjoy.	(a) Take a day off in January and decide what things are important to me in a job. (b) Find a good Life Coach before the end of January to help me plan my future career path.
6 Be happy.	(a) Lie in bed for 5 minutes when I wake up in the morning and think of three things I am grateful for. (b) Do one small thing each day (that I don't have to do) to make another person happy.

It is important that your intentions and targets are expressed in a positive way. For example: feel calm and relaxed, *not* feel less stressed. Simply setting these intentions clearly and writing them down will have a powerful effect on your unconscious mind.

Targets that are achievable are better than those you would find very hard to achieve. Targets should be things that you *can and will* do, even though they may stretch you outside your comfort zone. They should be SMART:

- Specific
- Measurable
- Achievable
- Relevant
- Time-bound

Gather whatever information you need to set clear and specific targets. Check that they are measurable and can be achieved within a specified time. Whatever you decide to do, make sure you do something as soon as possible to commit yourself to action. For example, it could be as easy as booking an appointment or telling all your friends what you are going to do. Start putting your plan into action *now*. Do your best to achieve your targets. Try to overcome any difficulties that you encounter, and at the same time, be aware of any anxiety or panic that arises. Simply witness any emotions and try not to let them stop you from achieving your target. (We will cover this in more detail later in this chapter.)

You can look at your action plan as often as you like. In practice, once per week should be sufficient, but you may like to review your progress more systematically on a monthly basis. As your vision manifests itself and you begin to achieve your goals, you may need to create new intentions.

Eventually, though, the number of intentions you set should reduce to just one or two that you still need to work on. Even when you are perfectly happy and fulfilled, it is important to avoid becoming complacent and to continue to review your plan in the context of what is happening around you.

A journey of a thousand miles begins with the very first step.
Lao-tzu (Chinese philosopher, fourth century BC)

Act selflessly

You will be keen to achieve your intentions and targets outlined in your Action Plan. Sometimes you will need to make difficult decisions about what you do and what you don't do. This will mean being firm with other people, but it does not mean that you should act in a selfish way. Try to find ways of meeting your targets in a ways that support and create opportunities for others. You will find that this approach will bring benefits to yourself and those you interact with. Do not become obsessed with meeting your targets at the expense of other people's wellbeing. It is good to achieve your goals, but the process by which you achieve them is far more important. The whole point of transforming your life is to become more actualized as a person in both practical and spiritual terms. Have clarity of vision and clear intentions, but be flexible and patient enough to respond to the flow of life in the direction it takes you. Universal intelligence knows better than you what you need and how to meet those needs. Try to focus on doing the things that make you and other people happy.

Set thy heart upon thy work, but never on its reward, but never cease to work.
Bhagavad Gita

Be persistent

Studies have shown that persistence is one of the most important qualities needed to be successful in anything one does. Persistence involves a determination to succeed and patience to move past resistance and failures when they occur. Clarity creates the determination and power to act; persistence and patience create the power to succeed. Therefore, you need to develop persistence in order to change anything significant in your life. Here are some tips on how to do this:

- Make sure you are clear why you intend to do something. How important is it to you? Is what you are doing consistent with your true self and your vision of the future? In order to be persistent, you need to raise the stakes regarding what you are doing. The more important something is to you, the more likely you are to persist in achieving it. If you feel like giving up, ask yourself whether your heart is in what you are doing. If it isn't, the sooner you quit, the better.
- Create the maximum amount of leverage to succeed by writing down all the advantages you will gain by succeeding and decide how you will deal with any obstacles to success.
- See problems as an opportunity for growth. See failure as an opportunity to learn how to do something better. You may need to change your tactics, the way you approach a situation, or your attitude. If you fail, keep trying new approaches until you succeed. If you are not failing at all, you are probably not trying hard enough!
- If a relationship that is important to you is not working, don't give up. Try a different approach. Ask yourself what is important to the other person and change your behaviour accordingly. Give the other person as much space as he or she needs. Never harass him or her. There is a thin line between persistence and harassment.

- It is better to love and be rejected than not to love at all. If you don't try, you will never know what could have been.
- Face your fears and do it anyway. What does it matter if, on occasion, you end up looking silly?
- Reward yourself for trying, not for success or failure. Don't worry about the outcome. Worrying causes you to become immobilised and serves little purpose.

When you have exhausted all possibilities, remember this: you haven't!
Thomas Edison

Look for good role models

Good role models are people who possess the qualities that you would like to develop. They are people who can help you become more effective in your life. If you want to be an excellent manager, one of the easiest ways to achieve this is to work for or with an excellent manager. The same applies to any other attribute you want to attract into your life. If you spend time with another person you like and respect, his or her habits and behaviours will rub off on you. A lot of this will be subconscious and requires little effort on your part. Role models can be parents (if you are lucky), good teachers, friends, celebrities, work colleagues, or historical figures.

If you want to be a good pianist, make sure you find a good piano teacher. Read about the lives of great composers you admire and go to performances of the type of music you wish to play. But beware: it is easy to become influenced by negative role models - for example, gang leaders, excessively thin models, and ruthless businessmen. You need to avoid looking up to such people. Young people who have been brought up in dysfunctional families may be badly influenced in their childhood and teenage years, and it is only when they are exposed to more positive influences in their lives that they have the opportunity to change in a constructive way.

Imagine for yourself a character, a model personality, whose example you determine to follow, in private as well as in public.
Epitetus, Greek speaking Stoic philosopher (55 -135 AD)

Network

Making contact and networking with people who have similar aims as you is a powerful way of sharing ideas and creating new initiatives. Networking is widely used by both business and individuals. Examples of networks include:

- facebook.com
- linkedin.com
- meetup.com
- utube.com
- blogs
- business breakfast meetings
- conferences
- specific interest or activity groups

Networking is not new, but it has taken on a new dimension in the twenty first century. Many people promote their ideas and business using the Internet and by social networking. Ask yourself how you can use networking to help fulfil your vision and intentions outlined in your action plan.

Networking is the new freedom, the new democracy: a new form of happiness.
Robert Muller, Assistant Secretary-General for forty years, United Nations

Declutter your life

It is great to have an action plan, but can you find the time to carry it out? Chances are that you are busy most of the time with family duties, work, and social activities that have taken over your life. If you are going to be successful at changing your life, you must change your habits. This was covered in detail in the previous chapter, but there is something else you must do *now:* get rid of the clutter in your life. By this, I mean the physical things that you collect, hoard, and surround yourself with.

Many of these things will relate to past activities and patterns of behaviour that you may be trying to change. They represent your old personality. It is an interesting fact that you can tell more about a person's personality by looking round their house than you can glean from a job interview! To change your life, you need to change your identity. And the first thing you must do is to get rid of the physical clutter that surrounds you. Physical clutter causes mental, emotional, and spiritual clutter. It can prevent you from moving forward. Make sure that the material things you own don't own you! Remove the clutter and make room for the way you intend to live.

Exercise 35: Declutter your life

Start by making sure you tidy up after you finish jobs. Don't let the washing up accumulate or leave books and clothing strewn all over the house. Go through all the old files, books, and magazines that you have accumulated. Decide which ones you no longer use - the ones that sit on the shelves year after year. This might bring up some issues regarding things or activities in your life that you stopped doing but haven't quite released. Make a decision to get rid of as much as you can. Be realistic: don't hold on to things that you are unlikely to use again, and don't hold on to too many things for purely sentimental reasons. Remember, we sometimes hold on to things related to previous relationships because we can't quite sever that last connection. Holding on to old things can make it more difficult for you to move on.

Look through your cupboards, medicine chest, attic, and garage. Throw out everything that no longer serves the life you are trying to live. Keep asking, *Who am I now? Who could I be?* You will find that many of the things you have hoarded have an emotional connection. If this emotional connection brings up negative thoughts, you need to deal with these emotions right away by making a positive statement such as, *I am letting go of these feelings right now, and I am committed to moving forward.* Go through your wardrobe. Decide who you are now; get rid of clothes that remind you of the past. Maybe you want your life to be more colourful and exciting. If so, get rid of any clothes that are drab and uninteresting.

Don't expect to do all this at once. Maybe spend half an hour to begin with. Perhaps you could clear out one cupboard. Give yourself time to deal with the emotional issues that surface. Don't feel guilty about getting rid of things. Give things to friends or send things to charity shops. This way, you are continuously giving to the universe and opening up space for new things to come your way.

Once you have become skilled at getting rid of material clutter in your life, you will find it easier to deal with clutter at an emotional level. Start saying *no* to emotional feelings that you don't want to have. Your emotions are directly connected to your thoughts and how you chose to perceive situations in your life. If you choose to throw out negative thoughts, you will become more emotionally stable.

Out of clutter, find simplicity.
Albert Einstein, Theoretical Physicist (1879 -1955)

Seize the moment

Although you have decided to follow an action plan, this doesn't mean you can't deviate from it when opportunities arise. The more you act in accordance with your true self, the more new opportunities will arise spontaneously to help you achieve your higher purpose. It is important that you recognise these opportunities and have the courage to accept whatever challenges they present. These opportunities and challenges will often bring you face to face with who you truly are and challenge you to act accordingly. The closer you get to your true, higher self, the more life will challenge you to live up to this identity.

This identity is the one you are choosing in your vision of yourself. How you react and what you do when unexpected situations occur is a test of whether you are committed to becoming your true self. This is life giving you the opportunity to shine your light into the world. *This is your moment of truth.* If you don't find the courage to act in accordance with your true self, these opportunities will occur less and less frequently. Act in the moment, knowing that you may feel frightened, self conscious, or foolish.

There is a tide in the affairs of men which, taken at the flood, leads on to fortune; Omitted, all the voyage of their life is bound in shallows and in miseries. On such a full sea are we now afloat, and we must take the current when it serves, Or lose our ventures.
William Shakespeare, Julius Caesar, Act 4, Scene 3

Release your fears

It is all well and good setting intentions and targets, but what do you do if you can't achieve them? And what if opportunities arise, but you are too frightened to take them? In nearly all cases, this happens because of underlying fears and emotions that are consciously or subconsciously undermining your ability to act. These fears relate to the three basic human needs: security, love, and self-expression.

Basic human need	Related fears and damaging emotions
SECURITY	Anxiety, panic, paranoia and obsessive thoughts/behaviour.
LOVE	Desperate for love and approval. Obsessive behaviour, sadness, grief and depression.
SELF EXPRESSION	Anger, desire to control others, feelings of inadequacy, guilt and depression. Lack of enthusiasm, confidence and persistence.

The following exercise is a powerful process for letting go of underlying fears and emotions that are blocking you from achieving your vision and the intentions you have set in your action plan.

Exercise 36: Release the fears that prevent you from achieving your goals

If you persistently fail to achieve one of your intentions or fail to take up a golden opportunity when it arises, you should carry out the following process:

- Sit down quietly and relax. Say your intention and the relevant targets out loud. As you do this, be aware of the thoughts that come into your head and any feelings that you experience. Do you feel any sense of fear or any other negative emotions? Stay focused on these thoughts and feelings. Ask yourself: does this fear relate to security, love, or self-expression?

- Allow yourself to stay with these feelings and emotions. Sit quietly for a few minutes and amplify these feelings. Get closer to them. Try to sense where in the body you feel these fears and emotions.

- When you feel your fears and emotions are at a peak, gently say the following out loud: *I release these fears and emotions. I feel secure. I love myself exactly as I am. I am free to be myself.* Imagine your feelings floating away in any way you like. Repeat this process until you feel more peaceful. If this doesn't happen, say the following words to yourself, *I accept these feelings and emotions exactly as they are, and I will release them when I am ready to do so.*

- You may need to repeat this process over a few days or weeks, until there is less sense of fear, and less negative emotions arise when you think about this intention.

Note: You can use this exercise for *any* negative emotions that you want to release. You may need to repeat the process several times over a period of days before you notice a significant change in your emotions.

If you still fail to achieve your goals after you have used this technique for a while, you are probably sabotaging your dreams at a deep, unconscious level. This is called psychological reversal. Basically, even though you really want to do something, your unconscious mind is stopping you.

This is usually a result of previous experiences that created a deep level of fear in relation to meeting one of your three basic human needs: security, love, and self-expression. If this is the case, and you feel incapable of moving forward in the way you want, you probably need professional help to release these fears. Therapies that can help identify and deal with these fears are covered in Chapter 9. They include cognitive behavioural therapy, emotional freedom technique and neuro-linguistic programming.

Some therapists believe that deep-rooted fear can relate to traumas experienced in past life lives. These can be released by using past-life review techniques. Ho-oponopono also deals with releasing deep-rooted traumas that are embedded in cellular memory or the collective unconscious. I think that these approaches can be very effective in dealing with cases that are hard to resolve.

Be courageous and resolve to overcome your fears.

Cowards die many times before their deaths.
The valiant never taste of death but once.
Of all the wonders that I yet have heard,
It seems to me most strange that men should fear,
Seeing that death, a necessary end,
Will come when it will come.
William Shakespeare, Julius Caesar, Act 2, Scene 2

Use your emotions; don't let them use you

Negative feelings about a situation can engulf you, and leave you feeling angry, frustrated or paralysed. When this happens, it is useful to review the situation that led to your negative feelings; the purpose behind this is to use your emotions to help you move forward, rather than allowing your emotions to adversely affect you. There are two ways you can do this.

- View the situation triggering your feelings in a different way.
- Use the experience to change your behaviour in the future.

The following paragraphs give some guidance on how you can do this for some commonly occurring emotions.

You lack confidence

- Maybe you lack confidence because you are trying to compete with people rather than accepting that you are good at some things and not so good at others. Try to celebrate others' abilities and admire them for their qualities. Decide not to compete with them.
- Make sure that you do some things in your life that you are good at in order to develop your self-worth in a positive way. If you can't think of anything, focus on something that makes you feel happy and persist at it until you become good at it.

You feel embarrassed

- Tell yourself there is no reason to be embarrassed, and feel good that you have the courage to move outside your comfort zone.
- Decide this is not what you want, and avoid putting yourself in the same situation again.

You feel disappointed at not getting what you want

- Reflect on the idea that there may be benefits to not getting what you want, or that you were trying to do something that was too difficult for you to achieve. If your disappointment relates to another person: accept that you have no right to expect other people to behave in a certain way, and that you don't want to become a control freak.

- Set more realistic goals and be persistent. Success is 90 per cent perspiration and 10 per cent inspiration. Talk to the person who has disappointed you; tell him or her how you feel. Don't criticise the person, but let him or her know your feelings. It is up to that person whether he or she will want to change their behaviour.

You feel lonely

- Ask yourself why you feel lonely. Is it because you have no meaningful relationships or friends? Or is it because you can't bear to be alone. Do you need to make more effort to create relationships, change the way you relate to others, or learn how to appreciate spending time on your own. Often, it will be a combination of all three of these things.
- Make a greater effort to be nice to other people. Find ways to give, in ways that make other people happy. It may be a smile, a phone call, or going out of your way to help someone. Don't always expect people to connect with you. Make the connection yourself, and allow them to decide whether they want to be involved with you.

You feel upset by what someone has said or done

- Ask yourself if you are being oversensitive or whether it is just your pride that's been hurt. If the latter is the case, decide to move on.
- Communicate your feelings without attacking or criticising the other person, and trust that he or she will change his or her behaviour in the future. If the situation reoccurs, you may wish to consider how you can avoid similar situations with this person.

You feel stressed

- Do you really need to work so hard, or are you substituting work for gaps in your life? Is work more important to you than spending time with your family and friends? Do you need to change your attitude towards what is important in your life? Maybe you were brought up to think you must work hard and be successful at any cost!

- Re-evaluate what is important to you. Take control of the situation. Prioritise what to do first, and be prepared to ask for assistance. Learn how to say *no*. Do your work conscientiously, but don't allow yourself to be taken advantage of.

You feel irritable or angry at another person's behaviour

- Look at the situation in a different way: perhaps from the other person's point of view. Put yourself in his or her shoes and try to understand their behaviour. Perhaps he or she has had a bad day or something traumatic has happened in his or her life that accounts for the behaviour. Can you choose to feel compassion instead of expecting the person to behave in a way that suits you? Can you accept the person, as he or she is, and choose not to be angry?

- Could you change your behaviour or actions to avoid being in this situation again? If someone is continually taking advantage of you or using you, tell him or her how you feel. And if nothing changes, avoid being with that person again (or set strict boundaries for your relationship).

You feel afraid

- Are you afraid because you have chosen to move outside your comfort zone to do something you really want to do? If so, can you face the fear and do what you want to do anyway?
- Are you trying to do too much? Have you bitten off more than you can chew? Or is what you are doing or thinking of doing just too big a risk? If so, can you think of ways to reduce the risk? If the risk is too great, can you avoid the situation? In many cases, it will be possible to reduce the risk to an acceptable level. For example: if you are frightened to give a talk in front of thirty people, you may be able to face up to this if you practise talking to a smaller group first. You could also make sure that you thoroughly prepare your talk in advance. If you are afraid of something or someone that really does pose a threat to you, then you need to get advice and help from an appropriate person or organisation. For example: in the case of bullying or harassment this could be a helpline or the police.

You feel guilty

- Are your feelings of guilt a result of what others believe is the right way for you to behave? If this is something you enjoy, and it doesn't harm other people, perhaps you should ignore these feelings of guilt and carry on doing it. In time, others will probably accept you as you are. Plus, it is not possible to have everyone's approval. It is more important to be yourself.
- Are you feeling guilty because you have needlessly hurt someone else or behaved in a way that is contrary to who you want to be? Have you violated one of your standards? If this standard is one you want to maintain, perhaps you should apologise for your actions or find some other way of redeeming the situation. If there is no action you can take to redeem the situation, view it as a learning experience. Tell yourself: *I will not repeat this behaviour again.*

Let's not forget that the little emotions are the great captains of our lives and we obey them without realizing it.
Vincent Van Gogh, Dutch post-impressionist artist (1853 -1890)

Transform your anger

I discussed how to deal with anger towards another person in the previous section. I talked about reviewing the way you perceive a situation or taking action to avoid being in the same situation in the future. Because anger is such a destructive emotion, this section discusses some other ways you can take action to transform your anger.

Although anger can be a very destructive emotion, it can also be used to transform your life and other people's lives in a positive way. It is often stimulated by a strong sense of injustice, and accompanied by a desire to change other people's behaviour. Used in the right way, it is a powerful motivating force for change. For example:

- Anger at someone who is abusing you can help you reject the person's behaviour. Insist on being treated with more respect, and if necessary, walk away from the situation.
- Anger at not feeling loved may motivate you to change your behaviour and attract more loving relationships into your life.
- Anger at being prevented from being yourself may push you to look for more rewarding relationships and be less dependent upon other people's approval.
- Anger towards people who are destroying the environment may be transformed into taking positive action. For example: by supporting or becoming an active member of an environmental campaigning group, such as Greenpeace.

- Anger at other people's treatment of animals can be channelled into working to help protect their habitats, improve farming conditions, or campaign against experiments on live animals.

Anger is a powerful emotion that can motivate action. It is important to avoid suppressing anger; instead, you can choose to channel it into constructive action. Decide to do something positive and *do* it. This stops you from being manipulated by other people, and it gives you more control over the situation. Once you know you are doing something positive, your anger will often subside and be replaced by a determination to change things. For example: if your child was killed as a result of drunk driving, you could become actively involved in a voluntary organisation aimed at preventing this happening to other children.

Exercise 37: Transform anger into positive action

Anger that is not released or transformed into positive action will have a destructive effect on your health and peace of mind.

When you have a few minutes to spare, sit down and ask yourself: *What makes me most angry?* Decide how you can use this anger to change your behaviour in an empowering way. Transform your anger into an absolute determination to act to bring about a positive change to the situation.

Include a positive intention on your tree of becoming and decide on specific targets to include in your action plan.

As heat conserved is transmuted into energy even so our anger can be transmuted into a power that can move the world.
M K Gandhi, Indian independence and peace activist (1869 - 1948)

Create emotional anchors

This is a very useful technique used in neuro-linguistic programming (NLP). It can help you release fear, anxiety, and anger when you are in a challenging situation. Instead of being frozen or overwhelmed by these emotions, you can switch immediately into a state of calm and focused attention. This latter state will enable you to deal with any situation more effectively. This is particularly important when you are moving into new areas of activity, facing new challenges and meeting new people. It is quite common to feel emotionally unstable when you move away from long-established patterns of behaviour.

Exercise 38: Create your emotional anchor for success

When you are quiet and relaxed, let your mind focus on an occasion in your life when you were successful at doing something that was quite challenging for you. Perhaps you were apprehensive about doing this activity, but by focusing on the task and being persistent, you were finally successful. It could be getting a qualification, playing tennis in a tournament, or going to a nightclub on your own. Try to pick a situation when you felt elated after you had succeeded. Now imagine how you felt when you were successful, *as if it is happening now*. When you feel that feeling strongly, create your success anchor. Do this by visualising, hearing, or touching something that you can associate with this feeling of success. Choose something (your personal anchor) that appeals to you. For many people, this will be a visual image; but it may be a sound, smell, or a sense of being touched. Here are some examples of the sort of things you might use as a success anchor:

- Touch a ring or a bracelet that you are wearing.

- Speak out loud a word that you connect with success.
- Visualise a beautiful rose.
- Imagine the sound of chiming bells.
- Imagine the smell of your favourite perfume.
- Imagine a champagne bottle.
- Visualise a hug from someone you love.

Whatever you choose will be your personal anchor for success, and it will enable you to reconnect with the positive experience of success you had previously. You can reinforce this anchor by remembering other successful experiences in your life, using the same process.

Once you have established this anchor, use it whenever you want to be successful at any activity. For example, you might use this anchor before, during and after a job interview. Trigger your anchor before you start the activity by reconnecting with the image, sound or sensation that you used in setting up your anchor. Reconnect with this anchor again at any time during the activity, especially if you are feeling uncertain at any time.

You can develop your own anchors for any positive state you want to create in your life. For example:

- Confidence
- Peace and relaxation
- Vitality
- Happiness
- Good health

You can find more guidance on the Internet on how to use anchors (search for NLP anchors). Anchoring is just one of a whole range of techniques used in neuro-linguistic programming (NLP).

You may decide to create a number of anchors to help you in various challenging situations.

Neither should a ship rely on one small anchor, nor should life rest on a single hope.
Greek philosopher Epictetus

Tread gently

I love this concept. Life doesn't have to be an endless struggle. Yes, we need to be courageous, but at the same time, we can be gentle with ourselves and others.

Exercise 39: Tread gently

Practise being gentle with yourself and others. By showing sensitivity and compassion for yourself and others, you create an environment in which both you and others can flourish and grow:

- Imagine yourself and other people are like plants that need to be nurtured and nourished in order to grow and develop their full potential.
- Do as little damage as possible to your environment.
- Don't be critical of other people. If you need to question someone's behaviour, do it in a gentle and compassionate way.
- Allow yourself to fail and feel good about it, even though you are not successful.
- Be mindful of your thoughts, emotions, and actions, and their effects on other people.

- Learn how to laugh at yourself and allow yourself to be vulnerable.
- Try moving in a calm and gentle manner instead of rushing around needlessly.
- Be polite and cheerful in your everyday contacts with other people.
- Constantly remind yourself that life is fun.
- Take time out to relax and do things you enjoy.

Nothing is so strong as gentleness, nothing so gentle as real strength.
St. Francis de Sales

Turn crisis into opportunity

The Chinese word for *crisis* has two characters that mean *danger* and *opportunity*.

According to Zen philosophy, it is the grit (*dukkha*) in our lives that gives us the opportunity to liberate ourselves. *Dukkha* may be translated as suffering, bitterness, depression, or a bad state of mind. *Dukkha* tells us that we need to do something about ourselves, and it shows us where and how to do it. By working with our grit, we can turn our suffering into a pearl of understanding or wisdom and transform our lives. We do not have to do this alone, and we can accept the help of good friends (*kalyanamitra*). In times of suffering, we need to let go of our ego and be open to others' help and advice.

The first step in dealing with suffering, or a crisis, is acceptance. Many people react to suffering by pretending it doesn't exist or believing that there is nothing they can do to change the situation. But suffering is always an indication that something is wrong in your life, and the problem will continue to exist if you fail to address it.

Write down the problem as it exists, and put into words what worries you about the situation. This immediately brings the problem into the conscious realm and helps to put it in proportion. Evaluate the extent of the problem. What is the worst that can happen? How likely is it? How can you minimise the risk? Visualise the best outcome you can imagine and decide what action you need to take.

Set aside time to review the problem and try to identify opportunities and benefits that could come out the situation. The more you focus on positive aspects of the problem the easier it will be to find a solution.

Success often comes when someone sees an opportunity where other people see only problems. Here is an example: following the decline of the wool industry in the north of England there were hundreds of unused derelict mills that were an eyesore in the landscape. Many people saw these as a problem and thought they should be demolished, and replaced by modern buildings. Fortunately, however, more enlightened developers saw here an opportunity to create prestige apartments while at the same time preserving the industrial heritage of the north of England.

It is usually not easy to turn problems into opportunities and often requires a lot of hard work as well as creative thinking.

Opportunity is missed by most people because it is dressed in overalls and looks like work. *Thomas A. Edison (1847 - 1931)*

Listen to the whispers

The intelligent universe tries its best to help us on our path of spiritual evolution towards happiness and fulfilment. Unfortunately, our mind (more specifically, our ego) tries its best to interfere with this divine communication. In order to tap into this divine wisdom, we need to learn how to calm the mind and observe the messages and signs that the universe gives us to assist us on our journey. The more we can calm the mind and allow ourselves to be present in the moment, the more these messages will appear. There are three kinds of messages we receive from the universe:

- Bad situations keep occurring or get worse.
- Good opportunities arise seemingly out of nowhere.
- Good things (or bad things) occur simultaneously. This is often referred to as synchronicity.

The third type of message - when events happen simultaneously - is an extreme version of the other two. When this happens, we are well and truly going with or directly against the flow!

Bad situations keep occurring

If we don't notice or ignore things when they start going wrong, the messages from the universe become louder and louder, producing more and more dramatic events in our lives in order to grab our attention. You might feel that your life is getting more and more out of control and things keep going wrong. You might become resentful, angry, or depressed instead of realising that you are on the wrong path and need to change direction. If you had listened to the whispers in the first place, things would not have got this bad. Notice what you were thinking or doing just before accidents or dramatic incidents occurred:

- What were you thinking about or planning to do?
- How were you feeling at the time?
- Ask yourself, *What am I not seeing or hearing?*
- Were you doing something that was totally contrary to your true self (going against your standards and beliefs)?

- Are you sabotaging your efforts due to inner fears and a lack of self-confidence? Most often, it is your thoughts or emotions that are sabotaging your life?

Either you are doing the wrong thing and you need to change your behaviour, or you need to release the fears that are sabotaging your life (see the previous section in this chapter, titled *Release your fears*).

My son, despise not the chastening of the Lord; neither be weary of his correction: for whom the Lord loveth he correcteth; even as a father the son in whom he delighteth.
The Bible (KJV), Proverbs 3:11–12

Opportunities arise out of nowhere

You are on the right path and receiving assistance from the divine benevolence of the universe. You are living in a state of grace. When you are clear about your purpose in life and have a healthy sense of self-esteem, you are ready to manifest yourself in a creative way. People you meet will recognise your enthusiasm and genuine commitment to what you are doing. Opportunities will appear without you having to force them to happen. You must take these opportunities as they arise. At times, they will only be whispers; at other times, they will be loud voices. You need to listen for the whispers and avoid fearing the loud voices. The more you live in the present moment and go with the flow, the more you will be given help and support on your path of manifestation.

Synchronicity

Synchronicity is when two or more events happen more or less at the same time (or an event takes place at a symbolic place or at a symbolic time). This is giving you a very strong message from the universe that you are on the wrong path or the right path. The same principles apply as in the previous two cases, but the intensity is much greater.

Synchronised events often seem to be impossible, mysterious or beyond belief. Here are some examples based on my own experience:

- You meet a person you feel a strange attraction to in a seemingly impossible situation. There is a sense that you already know this person even though you have never met.
- Something unusual or special happens, and at that same moment, you see graffiti scribbled on a wall that says, 'Carpe diem' (seize the moment).
- You are thinking of someone special in your life, and he or she phones or sends you an e-mail at that precise moment.
- You are cycling on a scorching hot day on a Greek island and realise that you have used all your water. You stop at the top of a long hill and say to your partner, *I wish we had brought more water*. Two minutes later, a lorry comes over the brow of the hill loaded up with bottles of water. As it passes by, a batch of six bottles fall of the lorry just a few metres from where you stand!

A young woman I was treating had, at a critical moment, a dream in which she was given a golden scarab. While she was telling me this dream, I sat with my back to the closed window. Suddenly I heard a noise behind me, like a gentle tapping. I turned round and saw a flying insect knocking against the windowpane from the outside. I opened the window and caught the creature in the air as it flew in. It was the nearest analogy to a golden scarab one finds in our latitudes, a scarabaeid beetle, the common rose-chafer (Cetonia aurata), which contrary to its usual habits had evidently felt the urge to get into a dark room at this particular moment.

Karl Jung, Synchronicity

Here are a few tips to help you receive the messages the universe is sending you:

- Learn to be still and sense what is going on around you.
- Feel that all your senses are connected with the world around you. The more consciously you do this, the more frequently you will experience this form of divine guidance in your life.
- Begin to notice what may seem to be small and insignificant things happening around you. Pay attention to any unusual coincidences that occur in your life.
- Trust your intuition.
- When you need guidance, ask for it from a divine source. Know that you will receive whispers, at times, in the form of intuition. Other times, you will receive whispers in the form of coincidences or synchronicity.
- Trust and act on the messages you receive. If you ignore the whispers, they will become less frequent. If you act on the messages you receive, they will become more frequent and provide a pathway to bliss and happiness in your life.

Coincidences are spiritual puns.
G.K. Chesterton (1874 - 1936)

Affirmations: put your dreams into action

- I am ready to put my dreams into action.
- I act selflessly to manifest my true self for the good of humanity and all conscious beings.
- I continue to pursue my vision in the face of opposition or failure.
- I seek out good role models to help me achieve my vision.
- I network with people and organisations to achieve my goals.
- I let go of all physical and emotional clutter that is holding me back.
- I have the courage to seize opportunities when they arise.
- I gently let go of any fears that are holding me back.
- I reflect on my emotional reactions to other people, and use them to change my own perceptions or motivate positive action.
- I use my anger to energise action for constructive change in myself and the world.
- I create emotional anchors to help me in my daily life.
- I am gentle with myself and other people.
- I see all difficulties in my life as opportunities for change.
- I listen to the whispers from the universe.

CHAPTER 8:

Enjoy and celebrate life

The seventh principle of conscious healing and transformation

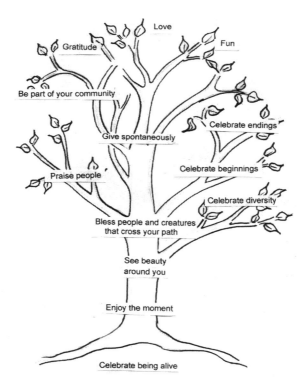

Verily I say unto you: except ye be converted, and become as little children, ye shall not enter into the Kingdom of Heaven.

Jesus, The Bible (KJV), Matthew18:3

177

In what way is this saying from Jesus relevant to giving thanks and celebrating life? Just stop for a moment. Imagine little children playing together; the way they jump up and down, laugh and scream and are completely immersed in the moment. Is this not life celebrating itself? Is this not the joy and love of life that some of us have forgotten? Is this not the Kingdom of Heaven? This is our natural state of being. This is the spiritual realm from which we came and the spiritual realm to which we will return if we can simply be our true selves and at one with all creation.

Celebration is a joyful way of expressing gratitude for good things that happen in our lives. It gives us the opportunity to thank people who have given us things we enjoy, share our love for one another, and give praise for things we have received (from each other, God, the universe, etc.).

Celebrating our success, the success of others, and beautiful things in our lives sends out a powerful message about who we are and what we enjoy. It opens a magical doorway that allows more good things to happen in our lives. The more we celebrate the good things in life, the more good things will happen to us.

Celebrate this moment

Being grateful for what we have and what nature has given us is a form of divine worship. Every now and then, stop and think about the things you are grateful for. You may want to celebrate some specific event, such as a wedding, a religious event, or the coming of spring. Or you may want to give thanks for being alive, for being capable of breathing the fresh air, for feeling the water from the shower gently caressing your skin. There are many ways you can celebrate life. For example:

- Make an effort to praise others for their actions and achievements (or for being who they are).

- Smile when you feel elated by something.

- Develop a sense of wonder for the good things in your life. This may be in the form of a silent prayer. You may wish to take time to appreciate the things that make you feel good.

- Celebrate key events in your life and the lives of others. Most people like to celebrate particular dates on the calendar, such as birthdays and festivals. Also, it is good to celebrate specific events, such as graduating from college or a soldier returning from a tour of duty.

- Find more ways to have fun and share your ideas with others. Look for opportunities to break away from the humdrum routine and act spontaneously. Don't take life too seriously; take every opportunity to play!

- Accept that pain and suffering have a purpose in life. This may be extremely difficult, but by totally accepting life exactly as it is, you allow the spiritual purpose of suffering to manifest itself in your life.

- And don't forget to celebrate your successes in bringing about changes in your life. This will have a powerful effect in terms of helping you consolidate what you have learned so far on your spiritual journey. It will help you set a basis for achieving even greater things in the future.

- Celebrate the things you have achieved in your action plan. You could do this by putting gold stars alongside the actions in your plan. I prefer to put a gold star in my diary on the day I achieve something significant and make a note of the details.

- Celebrate the fact that you have had the courage to do something you wanted to do, particularly if it involved moving outside your comfort zone - *even if you were not successful.* By doing this, you will make it much easier to take risks in the future because you will know that the important thing is that you had the courage to try. By celebrating our lives as they are (and accepting that everything is exactly as it should be), we allow the natural process of growth and development to occur.

Remember that you don't need a reason to celebrate! If you watch children playing, you will notice that they simply enjoy playing. Play is the most natural and innocent way to celebrate life. It connects us to the spirit within us.

The happiest man is he who learns from nature the lesson of worship.
Ralph Waldo Emerson, American essayist, lecturer, and poet (1803 -1882)

Be grateful

Gratitude is a powerful spiritual force. It is an expression of pure, unconditional love. It is the key that unlocks the door of abundance. By being grateful, you attract more things to be grateful for into your life. It also shifts the way you think from focusing on the negative to the good aspects of life. Whereas you may have been focusing on problems and obstacles to achieving your goals, practising gratitude will help you realise that the universe is continually helping you and providing wonderful and beautiful things in your life. If you are *not* grateful for what life has provided, you are denying that life continually presents opportunities and challenges that you need in order to develop on a spiritual level. This disconnects you from your source (divine consciousness).

Exercise 40: Be grateful

I would advise you to practise this exercise every day. Be mindful of the things and people in your life that make you happy and express your gratitude for some of these things each day.

You will find more and more things to be grateful for as you become more aware of all the people that contribute to your health and happiness. The same goes for the beauty of nature that surrounds you. Here are a few examples of how you might express your gratitude:

- When you go to bed, think of all the wonderful things that have happened during the day and quietly say, *Thank you.*
- When you wake up, feel a sense of gratitude for all the good things that the day is going to bring.
- Thank people for being kind, helpful, and considerate.
- Give people small gifts to express your gratitude.
- Write a list of all the things you are grateful for.
- If you meditate, or when you are quiet, try focusing your thoughts on the things you are grateful for.
- Remember the times that you have struggled (and as a result, become a better and stronger person). Think about the difficulties in your life now, and acknowledge that these may help you become a stronger, less selfish, and more complete person.
- Develop a deep sense of gratitude during the day for all the wonderful things that come your way. Feel grateful for your life, your home, the earth, the air you breathe, your friends, and all the beautiful things you see, hear, taste, smell, and touch.
- Be grateful for everyone who enters your life, even the people you may dislike at first. They often have a great gift for you: they enable you to develop qualities such as patience, tolerance, and compassion. Remember that everyone you meet is your teacher.
- Feel a deep sense of gratitude towards people you meet who already have what you would like in your life.

Celebrate their love, beauty, strength, patience, or other qualities they have that you admire. Connect with them and feel that you are part of them.

Being grateful for things around you has massive psychological benefits, particularly in helping to dispel anxiety and depression. By focusing on other people and beautiful things around you, you become less attached to your problems and your mind becomes calmer.

Gratitude bestows reverence, allowing us to encounter everyday epiphanies, those transcendent moments of awe that change forever how we experience life and the world.
John Milton, English poet (1608 – 1674)

Praise people

Praise is a wonderful way of recognising other people's ability, their personality, and their inner beauty. Your praise should be genuine; don't pretend to like something or somebody. We sometimes admire things in other people that we would like to have ourselves, and admiration can sometimes be mixed with a certain amount of envy. You need to practise giving unconditional praise, and celebrate within yourself the fact that others have achieved what you want (or have the qualities you like). By doing this, you are likely to attract similar things into your life.

Here are some ideas, but you need to develop your own:

- Notice when someone does something well, and say something like, *that is really good.*
- Notice handwriting that you find beautiful and say, *you have lovely handwriting.*
- Say to someone, *you have wonderful eyes.*

- Admire someone's way of dressing.
- Say, *you play the piano beautifully*.
- Say, *you are really good with children*.
- Write or e-mail shops, agencies, and companies who have done a good job and tell them so.
- Tell your friends and loved ones the things you admire about them.
- Simply tell people you like them or enjoy being with them.

And here is a particularly challenging exercise for you:

Exercise 41: Say something good

See how often you can find something good to say about people or things that you would normally criticise:

- Find something to praise about the people you don't like.
- Look for and focus on the opportunities that exist in difficult situations.
- Every time you want to moan about something, try to think of something good you can say about something or somebody instead.

Another version of this exercise is to see how long you can go without saying anything critical about people or things in general. You will be amazed at how difficult this. Moaning about people, the Government, the weather, or just about anything or everything, can easily become the way we relate to other people and the world. Not surprisingly, this is a slippery slope to becoming depressed, anxious and incredibly unattractive!

You will probably find that the things you praise the most are qualities you would like to have yourself. The more you praise and celebrate these qualities without feeling jealousy toward others, the more you will attract them into your life. For example, if you would like to have a special, loving relationship in your life, you need to admire and celebrate other couples who already have this. Can you do this selflessly and celebrate their happiness without any sense of jealousy?

Learning to praise good and beautiful qualities of people will lift your spirits. Love, gratitude and praise are the three key attributes that will transform your life.

Your depression is connected to your insolence and refusal to praise.
Rumi, Sufi poet (1207-1273)

Celebrate friendships

As human beings, we cannot exist without other people in our lives. When you were a child, you were totally dependent upon your parents. And as an adult, you are dependent upon many people. This is especially true of the developed world, where we are all dependent upon oil, food, and clothing from across the planet. In one sense, all these people are our friends even though we do not usually recognise them as such.

On a more personal level, friends play a very important part in our lives. Without friends, we are isolated and far more likely to become unhappy. As people become very old, their friends may die, which may cause them to feel a great sense of loneliness in their lives. Much of the suffering of very old people occurs due to this sense of isolation and loneliness.

Friends play an important part in our social lives (and quite often in our working lives). We usually become friends with people who share some of our interests. Ideally, we would spend much of our lives with our loved ones and our friends. Celebrating our friendships is great fun, and it is a great way to increase the bonds between people. Here are some ideas:

- Organise a day or night out with a particular friend or group of friends.
- Celebrate someone's birthday, an anniversary, or just have a regular get together with friends.
- Send cards and keep in contact with your friends when they are not well or going through a rough time.
- Buy little things impulsively that you think your friend would like.
- Say nice things about your friends in general conversation.
- Put things that your friends have given you where you can see them.
- Think of your friends when you want to feel happy.
- Let your friends know you are there for them whenever they are having difficulty in their lives.

Your friend is your needs answered.
Khalil Gibran, Lebanese - American poet (1883 – 1931)

Play and have fun

Play is a natural way to celebrate life. It expresses an exuberance and love for life. It is often useful to see your whole life as a game. The 'rules' of the game are to do your best, give love and respect to other players, and have fun. Life was never meant to be miserable. Even in bad times, it is possible to see the funny side of things and be grateful for the good things you have. Try to bring more play and happiness into your life. Here are some ideas, but I am sure you can think of your own ways of having fun:

- Focus on being in the present moment. Look for opportunities to have fun.

- Smile and laugh at things happening around you, and see the funny side to difficult situations.
- Laugh at yourself or say something humorous when you make mistakes.
- Spend more time with people who enjoy life, and avoid spending too much time with people who are always miserable and depressed.
- Think of things that would be fun to do (and do them!).
- Go for a picnic with your friends on a sunny day.
- Learn to enjoy and celebrate the simple things in life such as shelling peas, picking blackberries, doing the ironing, or doing the weekly shopping.
- Join in games with children.
- Buy funny toys and stickers.
- Hang decorations around the house at festive times.

As you develop a more light-hearted and playful attitude to life, you will be able to cope better with stressful situations. And you will find yourself laughing at all sorts of things that might have stressed you out in the past. Keep telling yourself that the whole of life is a game. Strangely, you will find that this will help you take on more responsibility in your life. By doing this, you are celebrating life - not only the good times, but also the bad times.

And forget not that the earth delights to feel your bare feet and the winds long to play with your hair. *Khalil Gibran, Lebanese - American poet (1883 – 1931)*

Come together and celebrate

All indigenous communities have ways of celebrating events as part of their culture. In a more sophisticated society we can too easily lose this wonderful part of our heritage. To be happy we need to be and feel part of a wider community. If you have a busy life, and even if you don't, it is important to make the time to participate in some community activities. For example:

- Neighbourhood groups concerned with local issues.
- Singing in a choir and at festivals.
- Dancing: there are a many types of dance suitable for all ages. For example: disco dancing, hip hop, circle dancing, 5 rhythms, salsa, ciroc, latin american.
- Story telling. You can do this with your children or join a story telling group.
- Music festivals.
- Art and craft festivals.
- Religious festivals.
- Community festivals.

The important common factor with all these activities is that they bring people together to share common interests and personal talents, and to celebrate being part of a wider community.

Identify the sort of community activities you might enjoy and plan to include them in your calendar for the coming year.

Always laugh when you can. It is cheap medicine.
Lord Byron

Keep a diary of your progress

At an appropriate time, buy a diary and a calendar for the coming year that fits with your personality and vision for the future. If you want to meet more interesting people, choose ones that have pictures of interesting people. If you want more romance in your life, choose ones with romantic pictures. If you want more adventure, find a diary or calendar with pictures of explorers or skydivers. Use your calendar to map out long-term plans that need to be organised in advance.

Exercise 42 Keep a diary of your progress

Use your diary to map out your next few weeks ahead in more detail, in line with your action plan. Keep a record in your diary of how successful your meetings and outings are. Maybe give them a star rating. I use a diary that allows me to see the whole week. It also has space for writing notes. I keep a record of things that I enjoyed, things I have succeeded in doing (from my action plan), and any lessons I have learned.

Look at your diary at the end of the week and ask yourself the following:

- What have I learned from my experiences, and what could I do better in the future? What could I do to improve things? What would I need to do to make these experiences even more fulfilling?
- What made me frustrated, angry, or depressed?
- What must I do in the future to prevent certain undesirable situations from occurring?

Keep a separate note in the back of your diary of things you enjoyed. And don't forget to celebrate the things you have done well in any way that is right for you.

Rise above difficult times in your life

It may seem strange to include this section in a chapter headed 'Enjoy and celebrate life.' Difficult times can easily pull us down into depression and despair. It takes great courage and faith to rise above these difficulties, and find joy and celebration again in our lives. As we go through life, however, many of us begin to realise that difficult times have a purpose in our lives. For example:

- Losing someone we love very deeply is probably one of the most difficult emotional challenges we can face. However, it may be that we need to develop new qualities in our lives, or experience new challenges. And consider; the person who has left your life may need to move on for some reason that is beyond your understanding. Celebrate the love you have for those who are no longer with you, but open your heart to new relationships and adventures.

- If you are suffering from a severe disability or chronic illness, search for the things that you can still do in your life. There are many examples of people who have done this - and we all have this ability deep within us. Steven Hawking was diagnosed with motor neurone disease when he was twenty one years old, and told that he had a life expectancy of two years. Since then he has become one of the most successful and celebrated physicists of our age. He has an amazing sense of humour, and demonstrates how we can rise above our difficulties and still live life to its full.

- Most people are upset when they are made redundant or dismissed from their work. However, many people take this opportunity to do something they have always wanted to do. They may take time out to regain their health or create a new business adventure. Quite often, so-called crises in our lives are the opportunities we need for our transformation.

No matter how difficult your life seems to be right now, celebrating the good things you still have will help you rise above your difficulties. It does require great courage and faith, but these are qualities that all human beings (and other creatures) have.

Celebrate beginnings

It is important to celebrate and give thanks for new beginnings in our lives. When a baby is born, it is natural to feel a sense of gratitude for the child that has come into the world, and to celebrate with others this new life and its potential. When we celebrate someone or something, we stop to give thanks and share our gratitude with others. Celebrating a beginning creates a positive foundation - either for a new life, or for a new enterprise that you are embarking upon. It sends out a message to the universe that you are embracing this new event or experience. This will create a loving energy that will nurture the birth of this enterprise. Here are some examples:

- Celebrate the birth of a new baby. If it is your baby, you could find a beautiful album and start putting pictures in it. You could put flowers all over your house and buy a beautiful candle to symbolise a new light coming into the world.
- Celebrate the beginning of a new relationship that you feel may be important in your life. This may be someone you have just met, or it could be the person you would like to spend more time with. You could find a beautiful card and send it to this person with loving words that express your gratitude for him or her being in your life. Or you might write a poem or a song.
- Celebrate the start of a new job, passing your driving test, or passing an important exam. Invite your friends out for a drink, or go to a restaurant to celebrate. Maybe you could treat yourself to a massage or a trip to a concert.

- Celebrate the beginning of the seasons. Every season has its own beauty and particular quality. Think of the meaning and purpose of each season, and try to bring these qualities into your life at these times of year.

You could even try celebrating a negative event when it occurs in your life! By doing this, you will allow the experience to have the effect it is meant to have in your life. In hindsight, many difficult times turn out to be important transitions in our lives. Remember, what you resist persists. Be still and say to yourself, *I welcome this new and difficult experience into my life and any lessons I need to learn.* You could do this at night before you go to sleep.

Celebrating a new beginning is like planting a seed in warm fertile ground. *The author*

Celebrate endings

Celebrating an ending is as important as celebrating a beginning. For example: it allows a person who is dying to leave this life surrounded by love, knowing also that those they love can continue their lives in peace and happiness. Similarly, by celebrating the end of a relationship, a project, or any enterprise, we bring it to a fruitful ending without guilt or recrimination. Celebrating an end of something is more difficult for many people than celebrating a beginning.

If we are unable to celebrate an ending we are still attached to that person or situation in a non-productive way. This can stop us from moving forward in our lives. Celebrating the end of something doesn't mean that we have forgotten the person or experience. In fact, it means just the opposite: we have put the person or the experience in a beautiful and loving place in our memory. We cannot always do this immediately when we lose someone or something in our lives. You may require a period of grieving to come to terms with the loss. It is surprising, however, how coming from a place of unconditional love can enable people to accept and celebrate an end when it has come. There are some extreme circumstances when this is very difficult, such as when a loved one has disappeared or been murdered. This is probably one of the greatest challenges any human being can face, and it may be resolved only through the ultimate act of faith. Here are some examples of celebrating the end of a relationship or enterprise:

- Celebrating the end of a career, a project, or the end of any sort of journey. We can nearly always find something to celebrate after any experience if we look hard enough. By doing this, we bring our journey to an end in a positive way. We cannot move on with our lives while we are holding on to grief, anger, or guilt.
- Celebrating the end of a close relationship. This is not always an easy thing to do if you feel angry or hurt by the way someone has treated you. However, you can *choose* to remember the good times and realise that other people's needs as well as your own can change over time. Increasingly, caring people maintain a good relationship with their previous acquaintances and ex-partners.
- Celebrating the life and achievements of someone who has just died. The more consciously evolved we become, the more we understand that death is a transition to another state of consciousness. Birth and death are intrinsically the same process. We cannot die unless we are born, and we cannot be reborn unless we die.
- Celebrating your own life as you approach old age. This is not something that we will all have the opportunity to do, and it is not always an easy thing to do. However, it is good way to prepare yourself for the transition from death to the next life. We all have different beliefs as to whether a next life exists, and if it does, what form it might take. I personally belief that our spirit moves

on from one state of being to another, although I have no idea what form this takes. We might choose to celebrate our life by spending more time with the people we love. We might like to review our own life and celebrate what we have learned, including what we have learned by our mistakes. Part of this process may be forgiving ourselves and forgiving other people in our lives.

Celebrating the end of a relationship or journey is like a tree letting go of its colourful leaves in the Autumn creating nutrients for new life to be born.
The author

Raise your spirit in prayer

Prayer is a powerful way of transforming your life. To be effective, prayer needs to go beyond your personal desires and the demands of your selfish ego. You need to see yourself as a vehicle for manifesting the intelligence and love of the universe in your life. It is not about asking for things for yourself; it is about asking that you may fulfil your true purpose in life. Use the prayer I quoted in Chapter 5 that helps you offer up your vision:

Bless me that I may
Fulfil my purpose on earth
And bring joy and happiness
To other beings and myself

The best time to pray is just before you go to sleep and first thing in the morning. Try to feel a connection with unconditional love for a few moments before you pray. Recall a time or situation when you felt this intensely. This may be a sense of love towards a pet, your children, or anything else that raises your spirits to a higher level. I sometimes imagine a picture of squirrels playing together in my back garden. What makes you feel a sense of unconditional love is a very personal thing to you. Say your prayer slowly and with conviction. You don't need to repeat it.

Prayer is not asking. It is a longing of the soul. It is daily admission of one's weakness. It is better in prayer to have a heart without words than words without a heart.
Mahatma Gandhi, Indian independence and peace activist (1869 - 1948)

Affirmations: enjoy and celebrate life

- I smile and celebrate the beauty, love and diversity of life that surrounds me.
- I give thanks for all the love and kindness I receive.
- I find things to like and praise about people.
- I create quality time for my friends and people I love.
- I am a playful and joyful spirit living on a beautiful planet.
- I look for the good things that grow out of difficult times.
- I celebrate new beginnings and endings in the same way as the coming and going of the seasons.
- I raise my spirit in divine love for all creation.

CHAPTER 9:

Alternative approaches to healing

Live in rooms full of light
Avoid heavy food
Be moderate in the drinking of wine
Take massage, baths, exercise, and gymnastics
Fight insomnia with gentle rocking or the sound of running water
Change surroundings and take long journeys
Strictly avoid frightening ideas
Indulge in cheerful conversation and amusements
Listen to music.
A. Cornelius Celsus

Healing is most effective if it takes place at all levels of our being. By this, I mean that healing needs to address simultaneously the physical, emotional, psychological, and spiritual aspects of an illness at the same time. This may involve using a combination of orthodox medicine, natural healing, and energy therapies. In my opinion, the boundaries that are often drawn between these approaches are not useful. Of course, there are many conditions that will respond well to conventional medical treatment used on its own. For example: fractures and other injuries may need first aid, surgery, or special medical care; but even in such cases, serious injury may result in severe emotional or psychological trauma that needs to be addressed in other ways. It is also important to recognise that recurring injury is often connected to our emotional state and associated behaviour. Examples of this include injuries caused by working under stress or resulting from intoxication.

Many less conventional forms of healing are effective because they help us to release emotional feelings and patterns of belief that are often the root cause of chronic illness. Apart from causing the disease in the first place, these feelings and thoughts can be the reason why we don't respond to treatment or relapse after an initial improvement. Once these feelings and thoughts are brought into the conscious mind, they can be changed in such a way as to allow healing to take place. These techniques, for releasing trauma and deep-seated emotions, can be used alongside conventional or complementary therapies. They should never be used instead of conventional medical treatment. You should always follow the guidance of your doctor or consultant.

I have only included, in this chapter, healing activities and techniques that I have experienced myself or practised with other people. There are many other therapeutic activities that I have not included because I have no personal experience of their effectiveness; that does not mean they are not effective. You may be surprised to see activities like 'Friends' included in this list; they are included because in my experience they can play an important part in improving our health.

Acupuncture
Aromatherapy
Changing your beliefs
Cognitive behavioural therapy
Emotional freedom technique
Five rhythms dancing
Friends
Homeopathy
Ho'oponopono
Mindfulness meditation
Modern herbalism
Neuro-linguistic programming
Spiritual help
Subliminal suggestion
Vital energy

Acupuncture

Acupuncture uses needles that are inserted at specific points under the surface of the skin in order to stimulate the flow of energy to various parts and organs of the body. The needles are extremely fine and the process is painless.

A slightly different traditional technique uses 'moxa', which is a smoldering cone or stick of herbs that is held over the relevant acupuncture points. 'Cupping', which is another traditional technique, is sometimes used for certain conditions; it involves placing warm glass, metal or bamboo cups over relevant points. More recently, electrical impulses, lasers and ultrasound have all been used. All of these methods work on the same basic principles.

Acupuncture is one of the most ancient forms of healing in the world. Stone acupuncture needles dating from about 2500BC have been found in tombs in Inner Mongolia. Acupuncture works by balancing the flow of energy (chi) that circulates around the body along 'meridians'. Insertion of needles at precise points along 'meridians' can stimulate the flow of energy and remove stagnant or blocked energy that is linked to disease. When chi flows freely and there is a balance of different types of energy, the body is healthy and free of disease.

What does acupuncture treatment involve

Diagnosis is very important in acupuncture and the therapist will spend a lot of time finding out where energy is blocked and the quality of energy in your body. This will involve asking you detailed questions about your medical history, symptoms, pains and sensations, and other information. The therapist will observe the way you look and the condition of your skin, eyes and tongue. She or he will notice the way you talk, and feel the quality of your skin and pulse. In Chinese medicine there are six basic pulses, three on each wrist. The quality and strength of these pulses are particularly important in making an accurate diagnosis.

During treatment, you will normally lie on a couch and be asked to remove sufficient clothing to allow access to the relevant acupuncture points on your body. The insertion of the needles may feel like a pinprick followed by tingling or numbness. Needles may be inserted for a few seconds or left in for up to half an hour; the therapist will manipulate them to stimulate or calm the energy flowing through that point.

Reaction to the treatment will vary. You may not feel any immediate change or you may feel re-vitalised, tired or 'spaced out'. You may even feel worse for a short time, as energy in your body adjusts and emotional tensions are discharged. Relief from pain and other benefits tend to occur after a few days.

The number of treatments you require will vary depending on the nature of your illness, but you should expect to see some marked improvement after three or four treatments.

What conditions does it help

Here are some of the conditions that may be relieved by acupuncture:

- Arthritis and back pain
- Poor circulation
- Depression and fatigue
- Digestive problems
- Menstrual problems
- Hay fever
- Asthma

Is acupuncture safe

Acupuncture is safe when practised by a qualified therapist. It works well with children and can be used during pregnancy.

Aromatherapy

Aromatherapy uses natural essential oils that are found in plants, flowers, tree barks and fruit. These oils have powerful therapeutic effects on both a physical and psychological level. The oils can be absorbed through the skin through massage, bathing, or the application of compresses. Massage is the most common way to use essential oils as it combines their therapeutic effect with the relaxing effect of massage. It is also quite common for essential oils to be inhaled using a vaporizer.

Essential oils can be taken internally, but this should only be done under professional supervision as oils have varying levels of toxicity and the effects are often rapid and intense.

Over one hundred and fifty essential oils have been extracted. They contain a wide range of complex natural substances. They have similar properties to conventional drugs but generally do not have the side effects of many drugs. All essential oils have antiseptic qualities. They can be used to treat viral infections, fungal infections, various inflammatory conditions, and to treat different emotional states.

Essential oils appear to work on the whole body system in a complex way. All oils are a combination of many chemical substances, and it is the combined action of these on the whole body that has a therapeutic effect. The aroma from essential oils has a direct effect on our emotions, as our sense of smell is connected directly to the limbic system of the brain - associated with our moods, memory and learning. Molecules of essential oils are also easily absorbed through the pores of the skin, and are circulated round the body to various organs by the bloodstream. Essential oils, that have important functions in plants, are also able to stimulate a wide range of actions within the human body.

What does aromatherapy treatment involve

Massage is the most common and an enjoyable form of treatment. Massage, usually of the whole body, is carried out using aromatic oils diluted in a vegetable base carrier oil. The technique combines the relaxing effect of massage with the quick absorption of essential oils through the skin into the bloodstream.

Your first consultation will last between one to one and a half hours, as the therapist will need to spend time asking you about your medical history, lifestyle and current state of health. She will need know if you are pregnant, have problems with your blood pressure, suffer from epilepsy or have had any recent operations. Occasionally, contact with your GP may be necessary, but your permission would be sought before this happens. Partial treatment, for areas such as back, neck and shoulders may be arranged and would involve a shorter consultation.

Treatment will usually take place on a massage table in a warm, comfortable and relaxed environment. You will be asked to remove some of your clothes to enable the therapist to massage your body. The therapist will discuss with you the oils to be used and ask how you like the smell of particular oils. We are often drawn to the scents that have a beneficial effect on us. Many therapists use a traditional Swedish massage technique but this will vary between practitioners who adopt slightly different styles of working. The therapist will not normally talk to you during the massage, as it is important for you to relax and be aware of the feelings and sensations you are experiencing. One of the immediate effects of the treatment will be the release of tension in the muscles and organs of the body. A full-body massage normally lasts between thirty to forty five minutes. You may feel a bit oily after the massage, but it is advised that you don't bathe or shower for at least four hours to allow the oils to fully absorb through the skin.

Aromatherapy compresses are good for relieving pain, reducing inflammation and for bruising. Place four drops of essential oil in a basin of hot or cold water depending on the nature of the problem (e.g. hot is soothing for back and menstrual pains and cold/iced is good for headaches, sunburn and acute injuries). Soak a piece of cloth or flannel in the water, squeeze it out and place it over the affected area. Cover the cloth with a towel and leave it for at least thirty minutes.

Bathing is an easy way to use essential oils in your home. You can simply add up to five drops of your chosen oil into the bath water (three for young children). Alternatively, you can dissolve some essential oil in alcohol such as vodka or brandy, and keep it in a container by the side of your bath to add to your bath water. This is more effective than adding the oil directly as it helps the oil to disperse more easily into the bath water. When it is not convenient to have a proper bath, you can bathe your feet. Add four drops to a bowl of warm water, soak your feet and relax.

Inhalations of aromatic oils are an excellent treatment for colds in the head, sore throats and sinusitis. Add five drops of essential oil to a basin of hot water (not boiling), cover your head with a towel and breathe in the steam for about ten minutes. Alternatively, you can put one or two drops on a handkerchief and inhale throughout the day or night.

Vaporisers can be used to spread an aroma around your room or office. A few drops of essential oil may be added to water in an oil burner or radiator humidifier. Choose an appropriate essential oil e.g. lemon or rosemary for activity, lavender or camomile for relaxation, tea tree as an antiseptic.

What conditions does aromatherapy help

The following are some of the conditions that can be relieved by the use of aromatherapy:

- Stress and fatigue
- Mild anxiety and depression
- Mild insomnia
- Cuts and mild burns
- Skin problems
- Poor circulation
- Aching muscles and joint pains
- Poor immunity

Is aromatherapy safe

Aromatherapy is safe when practised or prescribed by a qualified therapist. Some essential oils are toxic, but are perfectly safe when used in the correct way. Essential oils have a powerful affect on the physiological systems of the body, and certain oils need to be avoided when dealing with the following conditions:

- Epilepsy
- Sensitive skin
- High blood pressure
- Pregnancy

Some oils can increase the skin's sensitivity to sunlight and their application should be avoided before exposure to strong sunlight.

Many essential oils are fine to use in the home in vaporizers, in the bath or shower, or for application to the skin. For example: lavender oil has low toxicity and is particularly useful for acute conditions such as minor cuts or burns and to encourage sleep. Before using essential oils at home, I would advise you to consult a good aromatherapy encyclopaedia or visit a reputable site on the Internet. Do not take essential oils internally unless under the supervision of a suitably qualified therapist.

Changing your beliefs

You may be surprised to see changing your beliefs in a chapter on 'Alternative approaches to healing.' In fact, your beliefs are probably the most important single factor contributing to your health, and the most important single factor contributing to the development of your disease. Your beliefs influence your state of mind, affect your emotional state, and have a direct affect on your health:

- If you feel inadequate and need to constantly prove yourself to others, you will almost certainly suffer from stress. Stress has all sorts of negative effects on your health, including digestive problems, high blood pressure, and suppression of the immune system. Long-term stress can trigger many illnesses, including stokes, heart attack and possibly cancer.
- Eating disorders are nearly always connected to psychological and emotional issues. Obesity may now be the number one cause of disease in the developed world, and anorexia has a devastating effect on many young people. These are diseases of our modern society and are related to cultural and psychological factors.
- Depression and anxiety are prevalent in modern society linked to other conditions such as insomnia, paranoia and obsessive compulsive disorder. These are often connected with beliefs that we hold about ourselves and other people. In my opinion, many of these psychological states are a result of our sense of isolation from one another, and the breakdown of traditional family and community support networks.
- In spite of our increased material wellbeing, many of us feel insecure, unloved and unable to express ourselves. Security, love and the ability to express ourselves are important needs that we have as human beings. If we are unable to meet these needs we will gradually develop illness related to the areas where our needs are frustrated.

The effect that our beliefs have on our ability to heal is dramatically demonstrated by the so-called 'placebo effect'. Rigorous scientific studies have shown that believing that we have been given an effective drug can be almost as powerful as being given the drug itself. In other words, our belief that we are receiving an effective drug has a strong healing effect. Research into the placebo effect has caused major dilemmas for drug manufacturers. In some cases, the placebo effect of a drug under research has been shown to be more beneficial than the drug itself. It is also true, that if we believe a drug (or a particular food) will upset our health, it probably will. This is known as the 'nocebo effect'.

How can beliefs improve your health

So how can changing your beliefs help you to overcome your illness? This will depend on the nature of your illness. Disease that manifests on a physical level always has a psychological equivalent. There are many good books available that list various illnesses and their corresponding psychological and emotional states. You will find some of these listed under 'Recommended books'. The following list gives some examples of common health issues and some positive beliefs and emotions that can help these conditions to improve.

- Heart conditions: loving yourself and being gentle and loving to others.
- Digestive ailments: letting go of strong emotions and learning to accept life has its ups and downs.
- Eyesight problems: seeing beauty in nature and good in other people; seeing things as they are, in a balanced way.
- Hearing problems: willing to listen to others and enjoy various types of music/sound; being relaxed and at ease most of the time (not hyper-vigilant).
- Arthritis, mobility problems: open minded and flexible/tolerant of other people.

It doesn't take a great deal of imagination to extend this list. Every physical ailment has a corresponding psychological component. Your symptoms will usually tell you where you have psychological weaknesses that you need to address. Once you are aware of the possible connection of your beliefs and emotions to your illness, you need to work on changing these to help the healing process. There are many ways you can do this, but simply becoming aware of this connection will help.

Every time you observe yourself having negative thoughts and feelings that correspond with your condition, say NO or STOP firmly to yourself or out loud. Then say a positive affirmation to implant positive thoughts and feelings into your unconscious mind. For example: for a heart condition you might say something like; "I deeply love myself just the way I am and I am happy to share my love with others".

You may find it helpful to have a series of EFT (Emotional Freedom Technique) sessions to help change your underlying beliefs. These are particularly useful if you are not aware of what psychological or emotional factors may be connected to your illness; also, EFT will help you release 'negative' thoughts and emotions.

What conditions does it help

You can use this knowledge/understanding to support healing of any illness or disease.

Is changing your beliefs safe

If you have serious psychological or emotional problems you should always get professional help, and inform your consultant/practitioner of what you are doing. The process of changing your beliefs and emotions can be used safely alongside other types of therapy. For example: it is supportive of homeopathy and conventional treatment of chronic illness.

Cognitive behavioural therapy (CBT)

CBT involves changing the way you think about situations in life and adapting your behaviour to be consistent with your new thoughts. It focuses on problems you face here and now and how to deal with them. It does not focus on past experiences or fears you may have about the future.

A key aspect of CBT is learning how to stop behaving in a way that reinforces negative thought patterns or emotions. By gradually controlling your actions, your thoughts and emotions become easier to control. Your negative thoughts are like a dictator who controls how you feel and how you act. By refusing to act on his demands, you free yourself from his control.

> It is not possible
> to enter the house of the strong man
> and take it by force
> unless he binds his hands:
> then he will plunder his house.
> *Jesus, The Gospel of Thomas (translated by Hugh McGregor Ross),*
> *Logion 35*

My interpretation of this logion is as follows: The *strong man* represents the persistent thoughts and emotions that control you. *Binding the strong man's hands* means that you refuse to put your thoughts and emotions into action. By refusing to act on these thoughts and emotions, they will eventually subside (they have been plundered). This is the basis of CBT.

CBT is about choosing to take conscious control over your thoughts and emotions. It frees you from the effect of past experiences, negative thought patterns and unhelpful emotions.

What does CBT therapy involve

CBT can be done on a one–to-one basis or within a group. It can also be done by following a self-help book or computer programme. In England and Wales, the NHS has approved two computer-based programmes:

Fear fighter (www.fearfighter.com). This is useful for people with phobias or panic attacks.

Beating the blues (www.beatingtheblues.co.uk). This is useful for people with mild to moderate depression.

A general practitioner or consultant can refer you to a CBT practitioner, or you may arrange for CBT privately. Therapists vary in the way they practise, and it is important that you find a CBT practitioner with whom you feel at ease. You will experience something along the following lines:

- At the first session, the therapist will ask you about your particular problems and what treatment you have already had. She or he will explain how CBT works and how many sessions she or he thinks you may need. This can vary between four and twenty sessions at a weekly or fortnightly interval. A typical session lasts about an hour.
- You will discuss and agree with the therapist the problems you are going to work on.
- The therapist will help you identify particular thought patterns that are not helpful in dealing with your problem. To help do this, she or he may suggest you keep a record of your thoughts and feelings when they arise in your daily life.
- You will agree with your therapist new ways to deal with the problem you are trying to resolve. You will not find it easy to change your behaviour, but your therapist will encourage you to do this by taking one small step at a time.

- You will monitor your progress with your therapist at each session and develop new approaches that will help you continue to improve. Once you have developed an effective strategy for changing your thoughts and behaviour, you will be surprised at how quickly your problem is resolved.
- After you have finished CBT therapy, you will be able to apply the strategies you have developed whenever the problem arises. You may also find that you can use a similar approach to solve other problems that occur in your life.

What conditions does it help

CBT is a useful technique for changing any patterns of thoughts or emotions that are causing you problems in your life. It will help with the following:

- Anxiety
- Moderate and severe depression
- Phobias
- Obsessive thoughts and behaviour
- Irrational behaviour patterns

It has been shown to be at least as effective as antidepressants at treating many forms of depression and anxiety. It requires a strong determination by the client to change. However, it offers a more permanent solution to underlying problems without incurring the side effects of drugs.

Is CBT safe

CBT is perfectly safe. For severe depression, it is normally used alongside antidepressant medication. Tranquillisers should not be used as a long-term treatment for anxiety. CBT is a better option.

Emotional freedom technique (EFT)

EFT uses a combination of psychological techniques and acupressure. It is one of the newly emerging energy therapies. Although forms of energy therapy have been around for a long time, techniques such as EFT are relatively new; they were mainly developed in the 1990s.

EFT works by changing the energy patterns in the acupuncture meridians that are present when we think about an emotional or traumatic incident. The patterns of energy in the meridians of the body are directly affected by our thoughts and emotions. When we disrupt the energy pattern associated with a thought or emotion, it is impossible for that thought or emotion to be maintained. At the same time as disrupting the existing pattern of the thought, we implant a new pattern of thought with its associated positive emotions.

What does EFT therapy involve

You can use EFT yourself after taking a short course where you can learn the basic techniques. You can then explore using the techniques for dealing with relatively minor emotional or psychological problems, either on yourself or with friends and relatives. However, if you want to use EFT to deal with more difficult issues, you are advised to see a qualified EFT practitioner.

The actual process of EFT is very gentle. It simply involves tapping with the fingers on seven major acupuncture points at the same time as saying a statement related to your problem. This is followed by a positive affirmation that nullifies your negative thoughts and feelings. For example, Even though I was treated really badly by my ex-boyfriend, I still love and accept myself exactly as I am.

The EFT practitioner will repeat this process with you several times, focusing on any related feeling and thoughts that come to the surface during the session.

What conditions does EFT help

EFT is helpful for most emotional and psychological problems, including the following issues:

- Phobias
- Addictions
- Mild depression
- Anxiety
- Panic attacks
- Obsessive thoughts and behaviour
- Low self-esteem

Is EFT safe

It is safe to use EFT on yourself for all minor emotional and psychological problems. For more serious conditions, you should consult a qualified EFT practitioner and continue any conventional medical treatment you are receiving.

5Rhythms

What is 5Rhythms?

The practice of 5Rhythms is a life enhancing activity that encourages you to express yourself through dance and movement. 5Rhythms was developed by Gabrielle Roth to help people dance in harmony with their own bodies' natural rhythms. The basis for the practice of 5Rhythms is explained in her three books:

- Maps to Ecstasy: Teachings of an Urban Shaman
- Sweat Your Prayers: Movement as Spiritual Practice
- Connections: The Five Threads of Intuitive Wisdom

There is more information about the practice on www.5rhythms.com. A good video to watch on this website is www.5rhythms.com/life-changing-encounters-gabrielle-roth/. This video introduces Gabrielle Roth teaching the 5Rhythms practice and the benefits of dancing.

Gabrielle devoted her life to empowering people through the creative process; she was always clear that while the 5Rhythms is not a therapy it does have therapeutic benefits. She described her work as sacred art.

I have been doing 5 Rhythms dance for about twenty years and it has been an important part of my own journey towards freedom and health.

What does 5Rhythms involve?

5Rhythms is practised in groups that vary in size, and some teachers offer one-to-one sessions as well. The groups that I have danced with have averaged about twenty people, but I know of many smaller and larger groups. You can find details of teachers and groups in your area quite easily on www.5rhythms.com.

When you join a group you will be introduced to the idea that there are five basic rhythms that are found in all areas of life. These rhythms are:

- Flowing - beginning, finding our feet, and our fluidity.
- Staccato - shaping and expressing ourselves in the beat.
- Chaos - letting go, releasing tension, shaking out.

- Lyrical - exploring fresh, new ways of moving, lightening up.
- Stillness - finding the spaces between movements, moments to pause.

Each of these rhythms transforms into the following rhythm so that together they form what is known as a wave. This wave of energy flows through all aspects of life. For example: it can be observed in the process of planning an event, creating and hosting a meal for friends, and also in the cycles we go through in our lives. In Maps to Ecstasy, Gabrielle describes how the rhythms can be seen in the cycles of birth, childhood, adolescence, adulthood, old age and death.

Most people find that they like some of these rhythms more than others, and may have difficulty expressing one or two particular rhythms. But, by learning how to move in each of these rhythms, we can begin to clear blockages of energy that may be affecting our health and vitality. Our negative thoughts and emotions create stress in our bodies and become locked in our joints and muscles.

Most forms of expressive movement involve interaction with other dancers and this is particularly true of 5Rhythms. This interaction helps us to be more aware of other people's body language, and to learn to respect other people's needs in the present moment. 5Rhythms groups are normally very supportive, and are always run by teachers who have extensive training; teachers are trained not only in the 5Rhythms, but how to give guidance and support to individual members of the group.

What conditions does 5Rhythms help?

5Rhythms can help you to develop self-confidence through learning to dance your own dance and by becoming more connected to your body. It can help you to relate to other people through movement and self-expression without the use of words. In my experience it can help you:

- Become more grounded in the present moment.
- Express your feelings through movement.
- Relate more effectively with other people.
- Release stress that may have developed over many years.
- Develop the ability to sense other people's emotions.
- Feel connected to other people in the world.

When we relate to people in a group in a physical and caring way, our body releases chemicals such as oxytocin and endorphins that help us feel happy and relaxed. These activities also encourage feelings of trust and generosity. Needless to say, these feelings have an amazing healing effect on both our emotions and our bodies.

Is 5Rhythms safe?

5Rhythms can be very exciting, and at times you might feel uneasy, as the whole process helps to unlock blockages and tension that may have been housed in your body for a long time; at other times you might feel bored or disconnected. These feelings are normal; the dance floor simply mirrors back to you your inner self. The dance invites you to keep finding the movement that expresses how you are in the moment. If you are finding difficulty coping with your feelings after a session, simply try to accept them as they are without thinking too much about them; most importantly, keep going to the sessions. Generally these feelings will subside or transform themselves. If you need help, talk to your 5Rhythms teacher who should be able to give you guidance and support.

Friends

You might wonder why friends are included in a chapter headed 'Alternative approaches to healing'. The reason is that there is very strong evidence that friends play an important part in maintaining our health. Human beings have evolved as social animals and naturally form strongly bonded social groups. When we are having difficulty in our lives, it is usually our family and closest friends that help us survive. They may simply provide a shoulder to cry on, or give us practical help and advice to enable us to move on in our lives.

Friends also play an important part in social situations that help us feel part of a wider community; this applies at all stages of our life - whether we are a child, teenager, adult or senior citizen. As humans we have developed many activities that help us to socialise with other people. Most people feel much happier, healthier and more secure if they take part in a few community activities. For example:

- Taking part in community building projects (maybe projects like building the pyramids were an effective way to bond ancient communities together!).
- Singing in a community group or choir.
- Dancing together with other people.
- Talking about issues of common interest in an organised group.
- Eating and drinking in cafes and restaurants.
- Going to festivals and other community events.
- Taking part in theatrical activities.
- Going to sporting events.
- Going to parties.

It is perhaps, not a coincidence that people take part in similar activities in most indigenous cultures. This tells us how important these things are for society, and for the psychological wellbeing of individuals. If we have a few close friends, and are actively involved in the community, we are far less likely to suffer from depression, anxiety or any other psychological illness.

Ask yourself how often you spend time with close friends, and whether you take part in any leisure activities that bring you into regular social contact with other people. You may be very busy and heavily involved with people at work, but you also need a network of friends away from work.

Homeopathy

Homeopathy is an effective system of medicine that uses minute doses of substances to stimulate the body to heal itself. It focuses on getting to the root cause of any illness. When dealing with chronic conditions, it regards the whole person rather than specific symptoms; it also regards psychological and emotional states as being more important than physical symptoms. It often brings unconscious states of mind and suppressed emotions that are at the root of chronic illness into conscious awareness.

Homeopathy's therapeutic action is based upon the principle of *like cures like*. This principle was first recognised by Hippocrates, the founder of modern medicine, in the fifth century BC. *Like cures like* means that healing can be stimulated by giving a sick person a minute dose of a substance that would cause similar symptoms to the illness in a healthy person.

Nobody has been able to prove how homeopathy works, but there is strong clinical and anecdotal evidence that it does. It is used extensively across the world, both for the treatment of humans and in veterinary practice. Homeopathic remedies help the body's own vital force and defence system to re-establish harmony in the body. They work with the body's own efforts to heal itself. Healing usually takes place in the reverse direction to which the disease developed. Consequently, it is not unusual for old symptoms to reoccur and for emotional or psychological problems that have been suppressed to come to the surface. It may be necessary for these symptoms to be treated in order for healing to continue.

Another unusual aspect of homeopathy is that the smaller the dose of the substance given, the greater the potency of the remedy. This has baffled science - especially because the higher potency remedies no longer contain any of the original substance used to make the remedy.

What does homeopathic therapy involve

A practitioner will carry out an in-depth consultation in order to get a complete picture of you as a person before prescribing a homeopathic remedy that matches your specific symptoms. This is done because homeopathy treats the whole person rather than specific symptoms. She or he will be interested in the reasons why you have come for a consultation and will want to know a lot about you and what makes you tick. For example, are you very talkative? Are you always cold? Are you always thirsty? Some questions may be of a personal nature, and it is important that you feel at ease with your practitioner. It is worth thinking about the following things before you arrive at your first consultation:

- How would you describe yourself as a person?
- Do you have any psychological or emotional problems?
- Are there any recurring patterns in your life (e.g., bad relationships?)
- What makes your condition worse? For example, upon waking up, after a meal, during damp weather, or after exercise.
- When did your illness start?
- Do you have any peculiar sensations or unusual symptoms?
- Can you remember any particular incidents in your life that really upset you. Was there an illness or trauma that you never really recovered from?

After building up a detailed picture of you as a client, the homeopath will select a remedy that matches your overall constitution and personality and also relates to the specific symptoms you are concerned about. She or he will advise you when and how to take the remedy. The remedy itself will usually be in the form of a small tablet that is dissolved in the mouth. You should avoid eating for at least a half hour before and after taking a remedy, and avoid coffee and strong or pungent foods during the period of treatment.

Occasionally, you may experience an aggravation (a worsening of symptoms) for a short period of time after taking a remedy. This is usually a good sign because it indicates that the remedy is working and the healing process has commenced. You may also experience emotional or physical release as the body seeks to rid itself of suppressed emotions and toxins. Again, this is usually a good sign, but it means that you need to relax and may need emotional support. If the emotional release is very strong, you may benefit from other supportive therapies, such as Cognitive Behavioural Therapy (CBT) or Emotional Freedom Technique (EFT). These will help you release any underlying patterns of thoughts or beliefs that led to these emotions.

What conditions does it help

Because homeopathy works by tackling the root cause of illness, it is useful in dealing with chronic conditions that may not be responding well to conventional medicine. For chronic conditions, it is best used alongside conventional treatment. Homeopathy can also be helpful in alleviating many acute conditions. These include minor injuries, sprains, bruising, and an upset stomach.

Is homeopathy safe

Homeopathic remedies are very safe because the substances from which they are made are extremely diluted and can have no toxic effect on the body. Homeopathy may be used by everyone, including young children, elderly people, and pregnant women - although some remedies are not advised during pregnancy. You should make sure you see a properly qualified homeopath to ensure you receive the best advice and treatment.

Ho'oponopono

Ho'oponopono is an old Hawaiian practice of healing based on love, reconciliation and divine forgiveness. Similar practices were performed on islands throughout the South Pacific, including Samoa, Tahiti, and New Zealand.

Traditionally, ho'oponopono would be done in a community or family setting. The community believed that what was happening in their community was caused in some way by past actions of the community or its ancestors. For example: if an ancestor in the family was abused during their lifetime, the effects of this trauma could result in a serious illness of a child born into the same family. The healing process would involve praying for divine forgiveness for all current and past actions that have caused the child to be ill, and sending divine love to the child from the whole community.

In 1976, Morrnah Simeona, regarded as a healing priest or kahuna lapa'au, adapted the traditional ho'oponopono of family mutual forgiveness to the social realities of the modern day. For this she extended it both to a general problem solving process outside the family and to a psycho-spiritual self-help rather than group process. After Simeona's passing in 1992, her former student and administrator Ihaleakala Hew Len, co-authored a book with Joe Vitale called Zero Limits referring to Simeona's ho'oponopono teachings.

Extract from Wikipedia

The main principles to remember when using ho'oponopono as a healing process are:

- The only way of changing past memories and karma is by connecting with unconditional love to our spiritual being (which is also the divinity that pervades all creation).
- Everything we experience in our life is the result of past memories held in our minds and bodies. These memories form the blueprint of what we experience in the outer world. Our outer world is simply a projection of what is hidden within us. It follows from this premise, that if we wish to change our outer reality we must first take responsibility for everything that is in our lives. This applies to us personally, but also to the community and society within which we live.
- We need to ask the divine for forgiveness, and for it to erase the memories that caused the situation we wish to change. The situation that we wish to change could be illness, conflict or any other undesirable situation. Joe Vitale refers to this process as reaching the zero point; this is when we no longer have the memories that led to the undesirable situation.
- We need to acknowledge that our prayers are answered by saying thank you to the spirit within us, and at the same time feeling an intense sense of gratitude.

The spirit within us (which is centred in the heart chakra) is part of the spiritual divinity that pervades all creation. This may be regarded by some of us as God, Allah, Brahma, the Tao, or as some other representation of divine consciousness.

What does Ho'oponopono involve

You can practise Ho'oponopono on your own or be guided through the process by a family member or therapist. The process is always the same.

You can practise using this technique at any time and in any place. Use it when negative thoughts come to mind, or when events that you dislike keep reappearing in your life. Simply follow the following procedure:

- Imagine something that connects you to a feeling of divinity or universal peace. This will be something personal to you. For example: a pet that you love, a beautiful wood full of bluebells or being in a church or cathedral. Say out loud, *I love you,* and sense that you are radiating love from your heart.
- Now gently focus your attention on the situation you want to resolve. This could be a relationship problem, an illness or any other problem. Say, *I am sorry (that we have created this problem)* and accept full responsibility for it.
- Say, *please forgive us,* believing that divine consciousness will clear the memories that have created this experience from your mind and energy body, and the minds and energy bodies of all other beings.
- Say, *thank you,* knowing that that the problem has been released in yourself and all other beings.

Remember the simple mantra:

I love you. I'm sorry. Please forgive us. Thank you

If you look carefully you will see a close parallel to the Lords Prayer from the Bible (KJV), Matthew 6: 9-13

I love you	Our father that art in heaven, hallowed be thy name
I'm sorry. Please forgive us	And forgive us our debts, as we forgive our debtors
Thank you	Amen (so be it)

What conditions does Ho'oponopono help

Ho'oponopono is a process for releasing memories that are stored in our unconscious minds and the cells of our bodies. It can be used to release memories associated with trauma. It is useful when other approaches seem to have no effect, suggesting that the root cause of an illness or problem may be karmic. This will often be the case with inherited illnesses and inherited patterns of behaviour that are a product of the communities and society in which we live.

Is Ho'oponopono safe

Ho'oponopono should be used to bring happiness and peace to other people in your life as well as yourself. Used in this way, you can only experience positive benefits from this process.

Mindfulness meditation

Mindfulness is being totally present in the moment. It is an essential aspect of Buddhist and Zen meditation. These practices use awareness of the breath to help still the mind and focus the attention on the present moment. Thoughts and emotions are allowed to come and go without analysis or judgement. Gradually, thoughts and emotions begin to subside and are replaced by a deep feeling of calm and peace.

Mindfulness based meditation has been found to be particularly useful for relieving anxiety, obsessive patterns of thinking, and depression. It allows us to become free of negative thoughts and emotions by being aware that these only exist in our mind. We can *choose* to let them go. There is clear scientific evidence of the effects of meditation on brain activity. These effects can be summarised as follows:

- A greater sense of unity and wholeness due to increased activity in the right side of the cerebral cortex.
- A deep sense of stillness in the mind and difficulty describing this experience due to decreased activity in the left side of the cerebral cortex.
- A reduced awareness of space, time, and the boundary between self and non-self due to decreased activity in the parietal lobe.
- A blissful and peaceful feeling of calm due to stimulus of the parasympathetic system (which induces relaxation).
- A clear and alert state of mind due to stimulation of the sympathetic nervous system (which induces arousal).

What does mindfulness meditation involve

One of the best ways to learn to meditate is to join a Buddhist meditation group. You will be made very welcome, and you don't need to agree with Buddhist philosophy to go to meditation sessions. Buddhist philosophy embraces love and compassion towards all living beings, and this is an ideal state of mind to have when approaching meditation. Meditation has been practised in Buddhist monasteries for thousands of years, and Buddhist monks are well qualified to guide you through the process. You can also find therapeutic practitioners who are qualified in mindfulness meditation and use this as part of their healing practice. They may organise group meditation sessions. Alternatively you can learn to meditate on your own. You will find lots of good videos and information on the Internet to help you get started. Here is some simple guidance on how to practise:

Start by meditating for ten, fifteen, or twenty minutes. Try to get into a regular routine for your sessions, but don't make them into a chore. You should look forward to this time to be quiet and at peace with yourself.

- Find a quiet and warm place to sit, either in a chair or on a cushion on the floor. Have your hands gently resting together in your lap. Make sure you are sitting comfortably with your back straight and your shoulders and neck relaxed. Become aware of your body sitting in the chair or on the floor and of any pains or bodily sensations. Say to you self, *I am fully present here and now in this space.*

- Now focus your attention on your breathing and the sensation of air moving in and out of your body as you breathe. Feel your belly rise and fall, the air entering your nostrils, and the air leaving your mouth. Be aware of any changes in your breathing, but don't try to control your breath in any way.

- Watch every thought come and go, whether it is a worry, fear, or hope. When thoughts come up in your mind, don't ignore or suppress them - simply observe them. Remain calm, and continue to be aware of your breathing. If you find yourself getting carried away with your thoughts, make a note of them and allow them to drift away like clouds passing overhead. Return your attention to your breathing. Develop a sense of curiosity. For example: *there's that same thought again. That's interesting.* See yourself as an impartial observer looking on without becoming involved.

- When you have come to the end of your meditation, sit for a minute or two to become aware of where you are. Get up gradually and try to remain in a state of peace and tranquility.

What conditions can mindfulness meditation help

Mindfulness meditation will help you be more relaxed while at the same time improving your ability to focus on what you are doing. As you continue to practise, you will generally feel more at peace with yourself and other people in your life. Mindfulness meditation has been recognised by the medical profession as beneficial to people suffering from emotional and psychological conditions. It can help people suffering from the following ailments:

- Stress and anxiety
- Depression
- Obsessive thoughts
- Attention deficit disorder
- Hyperactivity

Mindfulness meditation will also help improve your physical health in many ways, including the functioning of your immune system.

Meditation was originally developed as a spiritual practice. If you practise it diligently over a period of time, it will help you discover your true nature and your relationship with all other beings and creation.

Is mindfulness meditation safe

Mindfulness meditation is safe. If you have a serious emotional or psychological condition, it would be wise to practise under the guidance of a qualified practitioner and to continue with any medical treatment and advice you are currently receiving.

Modern herbalism

Modern herbalism uses traditional knowledge handed down from different cultures in the world that have used plants and trees to cure disease for thousands of years. It combines this knowledge with scientific understanding about the composition and action of plants, and the physiological functions of the body. Herbal remedies are prescribed to be taken internally or to be applied to the skin. They are used in many forms, including tablets, tinctures, infusions (teas), decoctions (boiled in water), and compresses.

I am using the term modern herbalism here to distinguish it from non-western traditions such as Chinese herbal medicine. There have been warnings about the contamination of Chinese herbal medicines by heavy metals. These medicines also make use of animal products, sometimes from highly endangered species; apart from the unethical nature of these products I believe this practice may attract bad karma.

Many of the modern medicines we use today were originally derived from herbs. For example: aspirin is found in willow bark, and digitoxin and digoxin used to regulate the heart are found in foxgloves. But there are major differences in the way modern drugs and herbs work. Drugs are isolated from substances that make up a plant, while herbal remedies are complex combinations of naturally occurring substances. Herbs may contain vitamins, minerals, carbohydrates, trace elements, tannins, bitters, volatile oils, mucilage, glycosides, saponins and alkaloids. Herbalists believe that it is this combination of substances in the proportions found in plants that give the herbs their healing qualities. It may be that this combination of substances has a more holistic effect on the functioning of the body's systems than individual drugs.

What does modern herbalism involve

Practitioners in herbalism vary in their background and medical knowledge.

In the United Kingdom, medical herbalists who belong to the National Institute for Medical Herbalists, are trained in orthodox medicine as well as having a scientific understanding of the affect of herbs on the body.

Other practitioners base their work more on traditional knowledge and practice.

Herbalists often prescribe to support body systems rather than to relieve symptoms of disease. While it is not possible to say precisely how herbs work, there is a lot of evidence from clinical trials to support the effectiveness of herbs in treating certain conditions.

It is possible to buy many herbal medicines and plant tinctures from health food shops and on the Internet, and there is plenty of information in books and on-line about the use of these remedies.

What conditions does modern herbalism help

Herbal remedies are available to treat a wide range of health problems, but their effectiveness varies widely for different conditions. Here are some the conditions that herbalists claim to be able to help:

- Circulatory conditions such as high blood pressure, varicose veins and raynauds syndrone
- Digestive and bowel complaints
- Urinary complaints
- Inflammation and swelling of the prostate gland
- Tiredness and fatigue
- Skin disorders
- Mild anxiety and depression

Is modern herbalism safe

Herbal remedies are probably as safe as many orthodox medical drugs. Like orthodox drugs, they contain chemicals that some people may have an adverse reaction to. You should stop taking any remedy if you experience a bad reaction.

If you go to a properly qualified herbalist for treatment you should be given good advice on the dose and frequency for taking any remedies that you are prescribed.

If you choose to buy remedies over the shop counter, you should never take more of the remedy than advised on the product you buy. I would also suggest that you do your own background reading and research; many herbal substances can have a toxic effect if taken at too high a dose or for too long a period. You should always source your herbal remedies from a highly reputable supplier.

Neuro-linguistic programming (NLP)

NLP is an ever-growing collection of simple processes and techniques that can enable you to improve how you think, behave, and feel. They are based upon observing and modelling processes that have been found to be effective for particular conditions. NLP will enable you to:

- Do what you already do well even better.
- Acquire skills and attitudes to do what you would like to be able to do.
- Think more clearly and overcome difficult emotional issues in your life.
- Communicate more effectively.
- Manage your thoughts, moods, and behaviour more effectively.

Many NLP techniques work by reprogramming those parts of the brain that generate our subconscious thoughts, feelings, and behaviour. NLP also uses models for creating excellence in what you do. It does this by studying people who are very successful in a particular area of their lives and helping you apply the same approach in your life. This includes modelling very successful therapists, businessmen, and businesswomen.

What does NLP therapy involve

You can learn NLP techniques by going to various NLP short courses. This can be very beneficial because many of the techniques are fairly easy to learn and use. You can also consult a qualified NLP practitioner to help you through a difficult change in your life, or to overcome specific emotional or psychological problems. NLP will help you develop more successful attitudes and approaches to life experiences. These include:

- Focusing on outcomes.
- Developing new initiatives in your life.
- Anchoring your positive emotional states so that you can access these at times when you are upset or under stress.
- Overcoming fears and phobias.
- Reducing the impact that past traumas may be having on your life.
- Learning how to listen to people more effectively.
- Improving the way you relate to other people.
- Developing empowering attitudes and beliefs.

A practitioner will help you clarify what it is you would like to change in your life and help you to establish clear intentions and outcomes for achieving these changes. She or he will explain to you the techniques she intends to use and what you can expect from the therapy sessions.

What conditions does NLP help

These are some of the conditions helped by NLP:

- No sense of direction in life
- Low self-esteem and lack of confidence
- Mild depression
- Anxiety and panic attacks

- Problems with exams, driving tests, etc.
- Eating disorders
- Addictive behaviour
- Obsessive disorders
- Phobias
- Outbursts of anger

Is NLP safe

You can use NLP techniques on yourself for minor problems and to improve your communication skills. For more serious conditions, you should consult a qualified practitioner and continue with any medical treatment you are receiving.

Spiritual help

When we lose our connection with our spiritual energy and universal spirit (universal consciousness), it is like an electric toaster being disconnected from the electricity supply. Without this source of vital energy, we become weak, lose our sense of purpose in life, and may even lose our desire to live. Some spiritual teachers believe that we make a pre-birth agreement before we are born as to our purpose in this lifetime. This purpose will not be about achievement in a materialistic sense, but what we need to achieve in spiritual terms. For example: it could be about developing more compassion for others, dealing with unfinished karma from a previous life, or developing greater self awareness and confidence.

When we become disconnected from our spiritual source of energy we quickly lose our vital energy on both an etheric and physical level. This can also happen as a result of severe trauma in our lives when part of our soul becomes disconnected from our body. When we lose this connection with spirit, we are vulnerable to psychic attack and physical infections. Psychic attacks can disguise themselves in many forms. Here are a few common examples:

- Feeling the focus of hatred, jealousy or criticism: either to your face or behind your back.
- Being with someone who 'drains your energy'.
- Feeling 'captured or surrounded' by negative people that you can't escape from.
- Being hooked into a destructive relationship by guilt.
- Feeling taken over by some unseen energy form (demon).

When we are connected to spiritual energy (God), we are protected from these types of psychic attack. Our energy is so high that we either don't attract these situations in the first place or we quickly find ways of freeing ourselves from their influence.

Yea, though I walk through the valley of the shadow of death, I will fear no evil: for thou art with me; thy rod and thy staff comfort me.
The Bible (KJV), Psalm 23:4

If you follow the guidance in chapters two and three of this book it will help you to maintain your connection with this universal spiritual energy. Focus on creating love in your life and being your natural self and you will automatically 'plug into' the source of your spiritual energy.

Love all creation, both visible and invisible, and celebrate the fact that we are all part of one loving spiritual source. If you believe this, and put this belief into practice in your life, your energy will always be aligned with the highest spiritual energy that permeates creation. When you are connected to spiritual energy in this way you will receive protection, and guidance as to any action you need to take. If in doubt, raise your spirit with love in your heart and ask for guidance using the following prayer:

Bless and protect me that I may
Fulfil my spiritual purpose on earth
And bring joy and happiness
To other beings and myself

When you say this prayer, try and connect with a spirit of love and forgiveness for all humanity. You may find it helpful at times when you feel under psychic attack to feel the presence of a particular spiritual being. You will be drawn to these instinctively. On one occasion a beautiful powerful cat came to protect me when I was under psychic attack. Whether you call on the help of Jesus, the Archangel Michael or a Hindu deity, remember that all these spiritual beings work through the power of God and the Holy Spirit.

I can of mine own self do nothing: as I hear, I judge: and my judgment is just; because I seek not mine own will, but the will of the Father which hath sent me.
Jesus, The Bible (KJV), John 5:30 (See also John 5:19, John 6:38 and John 8:42)

Subliminal suggestion

All of us know that commercial advertising in the media is aimed at persuading us to buy and use particular products. Most of us also realise that the techniques used in advertising are often indirect and subtle. For example: very often a product is associated with other things that many of us desire such as freedom, a romantic partner or a healthy lifestyle. Although the product does not claim to provide these things directly we are enticed or 'hypnotised' to believe this at an unconscious level.

I use subliminal suggestion to help clients feel more confident and to visualize changes they wish to manifest in their lives. I establish with the client a series of 'intentions' before doing a healing session and include these indirectly in guided meditation. I am helping the person to dream the dream they would like to become 'reality' in their lives. I use this technique alongside other forms of healing such as homeopathy, cognitive behavioural therapy and emotional freedom technique.

If you are interested in understanding or using subliminal suggestion, I suggest that you study the techniques used by the American psychologist Milton Erickson and the work of the English illusionist Derren Brown. Derren Brown is famous for demonstrating how magic, illusion, hypnotism and subliminal suggestion actually work.

Subliminal suggestion can be a powerful tool for helping a person or people change their behaviour. It should only be used with the understanding and permission of the people you are working with. Alternatively you may use subliminal techniques to help change your own subconscious beliefs.

Vital energy

It is well documented by science that all living organisms have a distinct 'energy body' made up of pure vibrations: this is sometimes referred to as the aura, etheric body or vital force.

Russian physicist, Dr Konstantin Korotkov, and other scientists in Russia, Australia and Switzerland have carried out research into this vital energy. As a result of their research, we know that our energy body is the blueprint or template within which our physical body continually recreates its self. Kirlian photographs of the auras of leaves show that their auras continue to exist for a short time after the physical leaves have been destroyed. If the energy body of an organism is distorted in any way, this will cause some form of disease or deformity at a physical level. Distortions in the energy body can be inherited or caused by physical or psychological trauma in the life of an individual. It is also likely that our energy body is adversely affected by exposure to unnatural energy sources in our environment. These include:

- Contaminated de-energised water
- Chemicalised and genetically modified food
- Air pollution
- Electomagnetic radiation from cellphones and other electronic equipment

Contaminated water has a random disorganised energy pattern; natural spring water, however, has a beautiful vibrant structure. The cells of the human body can use the energy from clean natural water to vitalise their own activity. A similar situation applies to the air we breathe and the food that we eat. We need clean uncontaminated air and naturally grown food to vitalise our physical bodies.

Here are some things to consider if you want to increase your body's vital energy:

- The advice given in Chapter 3 of this book about being your natural self. When you suppress your own personality and feelings you block the natural flow of energy in your body.
- Spend time in the fresh air as often as you can. Avoid breathing contaminated air from traffic pollution and smoke. Have plenty of plants in your home and in your working environment.
- Check that you are drinking clean unpolluted water and consider whether you need to filter your water.
- Eat organically grown food where possible, consider growing your own vegetables, and reduce or stop consuming meat.

- If you are feeling depleted in energy over a period of time, consider seeing a therapist such as a homeopath, acupuncturist, naturopath or herbal practitioner.
- Learn yoga, tai chi, chi gong or martial arts. All of these practices involve working with the body's energy.

CHAPTER 10:
Reflections

Reflections on health

Promotes good health	Damaging to health
A clear sense of purpose and direction in life.	Lack of commitment and sense of purpose.
Highly motivated and enthusiastic. Gets things done.	Apathetic and depressed. Always put things off to tomorrow.
Feels loved and accepted. High self-esteem.	Feels isolated and rejected. Low self-esteem.
Loves and respects others.	Not able to love others (hard-hearted).
Able to express their own personality.	Feels suppressed and frustrated.
Able to enjoy being in the present moment.	Always worrying about things that happened yesterday or might happen tomorrow.
Feels happy in their relationships with people, family and friends. Sees the good in people.	Feels insecure and vulnerable. Always criticising and blaming others.
Able to understand and make sense of what is happening around them.	Permanently confused and disorientated. Sense of powerlessness.
Able to adjust and modify their behaviour according to the situation.	Rigid and inflexible (creates stress).
Have an active mind but also like to be peaceful and quiet.	Overactive or inactive mind. Never at peace.
Plenty of fresh air and exercise.	Lack of fresh air and exercise.
Plenty of water, good diet and eating habits.	Poor nutrition, lack of vitality and digestive problems.
Good sleeping pattern.	Poor sleeping pattern or insomnia. Tiredness and irritability.

Reflections on destiny and fate

Where do destiny and fate fit into the process of conscious healing and transformation? This is an important issue. If we are already destined to do certain things, or be a certain type of person, what is the point of trying to change ourselves. And if this is the case, is there any such thing as free will? I hope to throw some light on these questions by sharing my own reflections and conclusions on these issues.

I was once told by a wise woman that I had chosen to set myself a series of challenges in this life, and that I was yet to face my greatest challenge. I didn't want believe this at the time, as my life was happy and successful and I couldn't see why this should change. Many years later, after I retired from work, I suffered a major psychological crisis that lasted for four years. This was truly my dark night of the soul, when I confronted my worst fears and needed all my experience as a healer to deal with my own illness. From this experience I gained a certainty that spiritual help is always at hand in our greatest need. I remember this wise woman saying:

Each time you face one of these challenges in your life, it is like finding a beautiful pearl.

I see destiny as the dream that we choose before we are born. It is the seed planted by our higher consciousness to be nurtured and developed in this lifetime. This may be linked to our karma developed in previous lives. Our purpose in this life is to awaken to, and live, our destiny. It is not something imposed upon us, but something we have chosen for ourselves. It is connected to our spiritual growth and is part of the unfolding evolution of all creatures and creation.

To some extent our story is already written depending on where and when we are born. If you were born in Roman times you clearly wouldn't be able to travel around the world as easily as you can in the twenty first century.

But to what extent is the script of your life already written? I remember something a successful homeopath said at a conference I attended many years ago. She said something like this: *when you see a client the important thing is not their story, but how they tell their story and how they have dealt with the issues in their lives.* This is where free will comes into the story, and can transform it into a disaster movie or heroic epic, depending on the individual's personality and character.

Manifesting our destiny is not always easy. When we stray away from our soul's purpose, things begin to go wrong, and we suffer psychologically, emotionally and physically. Universal consciousness is telling us that we are not being true to ourselves. It is our destiny to become our true selves and to allow all other living creatures to be themselves. Following our destiny is not always the easiest path but it brings lasting peace, contentment and fulfilment.

In my view, we suffer fate when we are no longer following our true destiny. Fate is meant to bring us back to the path we have chosen. But the more we stray from the path, the more difficult and painful it is to return. Our worst fate is to die not having achieved what we set out to achieve in this lifetime.

You are following your true path when you are acting according to your true self and creating happiness for yourself and others around you. Your true self is not what you think you should or ought to be. To discover your true self you need to be in a state of complete surrender and open to every moment. Your true self will emerge when you are in a state of unknowing and you let your soul act in the moment according to its own nature. Let the universe show you what to do next. Be ready to go wherever the wind (spirit) blows. Be a free spirit.

Reflections on the Sri Yantra

The Sri Yantra is referred to in the ancient vedic scriptures of India, and has been used in hindu, buddhist and tantric traditions for thousands of years. It has similarities to the design of many temples and places of worship in India, and pyramids found in Egypt, Europe, Central America and elsewhere in the world.

The Sri Yantra is a powerful visual symbol representing the energy of creation responsible for both the cosmos (macrocosm) and life on earth (microcosm). It has four isosceles triangles with the apexes pointing upwards, symbolising Shiva or the masculine, and five isosceles triangles with the apexes pointing downward symbolising Shakti or the feminine. The triangles are of various sizes and intersect with one another. In the middle is the power point called bindu. This is the centre of consciousness from which the cosmos expands.

Image source: Wikipedia

Meditating on the Sri Yantra will bring about a sense of oneness and unity with all creation. It will help you to connect with your own inner consciousness (atman) that is a part of the universal consciousness (Brahman). If you decide to use this powerful yantra, I would recommend that you use it in conjunction with the prayer in Exercise 29:

Bless me that I may
Fulfil my spiritual purpose on earth
And bring joy and happiness
To other beings and my self

You may find suggestions elsewhere that you use this yantra for attracting things that you think you need in life such as money, success and the perfect relationship. I recommend that you never use it with these specific intentions as this will not bring you happiness, and I believe it is a misuse of spiritual energy. You can use it to help you connect with cosmic consciousness (holy spirit), especially if you are seeking spiritual guidance in your life. When you meditate on this yantra try to be in a state of openness, or submission, ready to receive whatever guidance you need. See the important cautionary note at the end of Chapter 5 relating to the temptations of Jesus by Satan to use his spiritual power for his own aggrandisement.

Reflections on enlightenment and the kingdom of heaven

Enlightenment is a state of being in which the individual is one with universal consciousness.

Enlightenment is not about obtaining personal salvation or escape from suffering and the everlasting cycle of re-incarnations. Personal salvation is a delusion. We are all connected to one another. To enter heaven alone is to deny our humanity and love for other sentient beings on the planet.

> Develop great compassion for all beings. Liking people is the basis for compassion. Develop an equal concern for others. There is no difference between us. We need to meditate on this. Think of all living beings as being part of one body. Meditate on the kindness of all.
> *Talk by Kelsang Kechogg based on the teachings of the Venerable Geshe Kelsang Gyatso.*

Enlightenment does not come by setting oneself apart from others. It demands humility and love for our neighbours. We should guard against any form of spiritual elitism where we view ourselves, or others, as spiritually superior. Jesus condemned the Pharisees and taught that only those with humility could enter the kingdom of heaven.

> Blessed are the poor in spirit: for theirs is the kingdom of heaven.
> *Jesus, the Bible (KJV), Matthew 5:3*

Many cult leaders, religious leaders and dictators have had a high level of spiritual knowledge and have used this to acquire power and assert control over individuals and the masses. This is condemned in the Bible as the work of Satan.

> Again, the devil taketh him up into an exceeding high mountain, and showeth him all the kingdoms of the world, and the glory of them; and saith unto him, All these things will I give thee, if thou wilt fall down and worship me. Then saith Jesus unto him, *Get thee hence, Satan: for it is written, Thou shalt worship the Lord thy God and him only shalt thou serve.*
> *The Bible (KJV), Matthew 4:8-10*

Jesus gave us two commandments:

> And thou shalt love the Lord thy God with all thy heart, and with all thy soul, and with all thy mind, and with all thy strength: this is the first commandment. And the second is like, namely this, Thou shalt love thy neighbour as thyself. There is none other commandment greater than these.
> *Jesus, the Bible (KJV), Mark12:30–31*

To love God with all our heart is to love all creation; God (or divine consciousness) is present in all creation. As humans, we have dominion over the earth and should exercise love and compassion for all creatures on the earth and the earth itself. This is also a central teaching of Buddhism.

Another aspect of enlightenment that is common to many spiritual teachings is that it is a state of being. It exists in the present moment; it is not a kingdom that will come into being at some time in the future.

> And as ye go, preach, saying, the kingdom of heaven is at hand.
> *Jesus, the Bible (KJV), Matthew 10:7*

> The kingdom of God cometh not with observation: neither shall they say, Lo here! or, lo there! for, behold, the kingdom of God is within you.
> *Jesus, the Bible (KJV), Luke 17:20-21*

> What cannot be seen with the eye, but that whereby the eye can see: know that alone to be Brahman the Spirit and not what people here adore. What cannot be heard with the ear but that whereby the ear can hear: know that to be alone Brahman the Spirit and not what people here adore. What cannot be thought with the mind, but that whereby the mind can think: know that alone to be Brahman the Spirit and not what people here adore.
> *Kena Upanishad*

241

This message, that the Kingdom of Heaven is already here, is the good news of the New Testament gospels.

Reflections on the ego

In his book, *A New Earth,* Eckhart Tolle describes the ego as a conglomeration of recurring thought forms, and conditioned mental and emotional patterns, that are invested with the sense of self. Most of these thought forms and emotional patterns are acquired in our early childhood as a result of our experiences. By the age of three, children have usually developed a clearly defined sense of self (ego). This programming continues throughout childhood and adolescence when it is influenced by wider cultural and social norms and beliefs.

A healthy and positive sense of self is necessary in order for us to function as happy and effective human beings within society as a whole. However, bad experiences in early childhood may result in a damaged sense of self. For example, prolonged separation of mother and child after birth (common in the West) allows two destructive beliefs to take root:

- Fear (the world is a dangerous place)
- Shame (I am not loved, and I am not good enough)

As a result of these early experiences, the ego can easily become fixed at the level of the child; and when we develop into an adult, we are constantly afraid of life, and feel inferior to other people.

In order to become a free human being, you need to learn that your real self is not your ego. You can choose to be who you want to be, and to develop the personality you need to be your true self. Here are some tips on how to do this:

- Accept yourself as you are. If you see any part of yourself as the enemy, you are rejecting part of yourself. This reinforces the sense of fear and shame you experienced as a child.
- Work gently with your inner child to alter your feelings and beliefs about yourself, other people, and the world around you.
- Learn how to let go of your ego and trust others and the universe.

In one sense, we need to extinguish our ego in order to experience enlightenment and unconditional love towards others. On the other hand, we need a healthy ego in order to manifest our particular light in the world. These two things are achievable. The important point is to observe Gill Edwards's advice (in her book Pure Bliss) not to allow the ego to run the show. The ego needs to be under the control of our conscious awareness, and we need to ignore it when it serves no useful purpose. We can do this by practising mindfulness and by choosing not to follow our first impulses when they are purely selfish or self centred.

Happy is the man who has toiled to lose *ahamkara* (ego); he has found the Life.
Jesus, The Gospel of Thomas ((translated by Hugh McGregor Ross), Logion 58

Reflections on the nature of God

The idea of higher creative beings that control the forces of nature and our destiny has been around for many thousands of years. Most ancient tribes and societies used the concept of gods to explain things that they did not understand and had little control over.

As human groups developed into larger tribes and societies, certain individuals began to claim to have particular knowledge or divine inspiration. These were the shamans or priests that had knowledge about nature that other less-educated people had no access to. Because of this knowledge, they were often able to predict events such as seasons and eclipses that would have seemed totally mysterious to the masses. This gave this elite group of people tremendous power over others. As societies continued to grow, leaders and kings realised the power of religion and began to claim their own divine lineage to God. For example, in Egypt, Pharaoh Akhenaten, in the fourteenth century BC defied the priests who controlled Egypt and maintained that he was the divine representative on earth of the one God, Aten. Although Egypt reverted to its old pantheism of gods after his death, monotheism became a dominant theme in many societies. Monotheism is characteristic of the Abrahamic religions (Judaism, Christianity, and Islam), Sikhism, and Baha'i, and it is found in the Advaita, Dvaita, and Vishishtadvaita philosophies of Hinduism.

It is important to distinguish between the idea of one God separate from creation and the idea that one God pervades all creation. Many people who adhere to and practise monotheistic faiths view God as a separate being that created the universe. But close examination of the scriptures suggests that the original followers of these faiths had a clear understanding that God, far from being separate from us, could only be experienced within us.

> If those who lead you say to you: See, the kingdom is in heaven, then the birds of the heaven will go before you; if they say to you: It is in the sea, then the fish will go before you. But the kingdom is within you, and it is outside of you. When you know yourselves, then you will be known, and you will know that you are the sons of the living Father. But if you do not know yourselves, then you are in poverty, and you are poverty.
> *Jesus, the Gospel of Thomas ((translated by Hugh McGregor Ross), Logion 3*

Advaita philosophy teaches that Brahma created everything, but that every conscious being is a part of God. We are all part of the great ocean of cosmic consciousness that connects us to all living creatures and inanimate objects.

This philosophy is consistent with modern quantum physics that maintains that all things in the universe (creatures and inanimate objects) are manifestations of energy. We cannot see this energy permeating all creation any more than we can see God.

When talking about God, we should bear in mind that we are postulating an idea for which there is no scientific proof. The only proof, as such, is the experience of mystics and ordinary people who have reported divine revelations in their lives. These experiences include:

- An experience of God consistent with one's spiritual beliefs. For example: if you are a Christian, you may experience the presence of angels or Christ in your life - this might come at a point of crisis in your life, as a result of silent meditation, or in another unexpected manner.
- An overwhelming sense of love, calm, and peace, and an awareness of the connectedness of all beings in the universe.
- A sense of being one with some universal force, divinity, or consciousness.
- An experience of time standing still.

It is abundantly clear that we cannot see God or divinity in a conventional sense.

No man has seen God at any time.
The Bible (KJV), John1:18

The only way to be convinced of the existence of God is to experience the effects of God in our own life. What we chose to call this experience is unimportant. In fact, the attempt to describe this experience in terms of a God is futile. This is eloquently described in the opening verse of the *Tao Te Ching,* written by Lao-tzu, possibly in the sixth century BC:

> The tao that can be told is not the eternal Tao.
> The name that can be named is not the eternal Name.
> Since before time and space were
> The Tao is.
> It is beyond is and is not.
> How do I know this is true?
> I look inside myself and see.
> *Tao Te Ching, verse 21, translated by Stephen Mitchell*

By being connected to the Tao (God), you become connected to the flow of life and the unity of all existence. In this book, I talk about being connected to our higher consciousness or divinity within us. This entails being at one with God. The first commandment, confirmed by Jesus in his teaching, is to love God with all thy heart. This can be interpreted to mean we should love all creation, including all other living creatures and the earth that nurtures and supports us. God is all creation and the unity of all existence and time.

Reflections on time and space

Modern physics has shown that, although we experience time and space as separate realities, they are dependent upon one another. One cannot exist without the other. We only experience the physical world and the universe in the way that we do because we live in three dimensions (four, if you include time). If we lived in two dimensions, the world would appear to be flat. We would see everything as flat shapes moving around on a flat surface. In order to explain subatomic behaviour, we now know that the universe needs to be viewed as having ten or more dimensions! This knowledge may help us explain a number of strange things:

- The reason why ancient Indian wisdom says that the physical world is an illusion (maya), and that we can only perceive with our senses those aspects of creation that manifest themselves (exist) in time and space. If we were able to perceive things in more dimensions, they would appear completely different. In this sense, what we think is the real world is only one way of perceiving things; it is completely dependent upon our limited sensory organs.

- In higher dimensions, things that appear to be separate in three dimensions are in fact connected. For example, it is possible that separate units of consciousness (you, for example) are part of a universal consciousness that pervades the universe. Hence, the assertion in many spiritual teachings that we are all connected to one another. Another way of expressing this is that individual consciousness is like a wave on the ocean. Each wave is separate, but it is part of the universal ocean of consciousness.

- Within the dimensional framework we live in, time is linear and appears to move forward and never backward. As a result of this perception, what happens today is a direct consequence of what happened yesterday, and today's events will determine what happens tomorrow. This leads to the law of cause and effect. But at higher dimensions, this does not necessarily follow. It is possible that, at higher dimensions, everything exists in the present moment, and that past and future do not exist. When you start to master the power of imagination and intention, you will realise that what manifests itself in the present often contradicts the laws of cause and effect. This is what most people call a miracle because it appears to contradict our understanding of how things normally happen.

- Because we can conjecture that time does not exist in higher dimensions, there is no longer any need to answer impossible questions such as what existed before the beginning of our universe (usually attributed to the Big Bang).

Reflections on universal truths

The Law of Infinite Oneness
An energy field connects everything in creation to everything else (this field has been called the matrix and zero point field, and may also be the Higgs field). The universe is an infinite hologram. Everything exists at a single point; it is everywhere at the same time.

The Law of Perpetual Transmutation of Energy
Energy is conserved. Everything continually changes form. Mass can be converted into energy ($E=mc^2$).

The Law of Attraction
All things vibrate at specific frequencies. These vibrations create resonance with other things vibrating at similar frequencies. We can attract the things we desire by manifesting their qualities within ourselves.

The Law of Creation
Our thoughts, feelings, words, and actions create the world around us. We have the power to create peace, harmony, and abundance.

The Law of Karma
Every action has an equal reaction. What we sow, we reap. The effects of our good deeds are peace of mind, happiness and good

health. Every person receives the challenges he or she needs to strengthen his or her inner light.

The Law of Polarity

Every thing has polarity (duality), except the origin of all things (the Tao). Things only exist because of their polarity. For example: good vs bad, light vs darkness, hot vs cold, positive vs negative, female vs male, and yin vs yang. Each of these things cannot exist without their polar opposite.

Chapter 11:
In a Nutshell

The key to happiness is to love what *is*.
The key to success is to love what you *do*.

To be is to do.
Heidegger

To do is to be.
Sartre

Do be do be do.
Frank Sinatra

Recommended books

Spirituality in the Gospel of Thomas
Hugh McGregor Ross and John Blamires

Tao Te Ching
Lao-tzu, translated by Stephen Mitchell

Ascension: An Analysis of the Art of Ascension as taught by the Ishayas
MSI

The Power of Your Subconscious Mind
Dr Joseph Murphy

Your Erroneous Zones
Dr Wayne W. Dyer

Feel the Fear and Do It Anyway
Susan Jeffers

Pure Bliss: The Art of Living in Soft Time
Gill Edwards

Conscious Healing
Gill Edwards

The Biology of Belief: Unleashing the Power of Consciousness, Matter and Miracles
Bruce Lipton

A New Earth
Eckhart Tolle

How Your Mind Can Heal Your Body
David Hamilton

The Divine Matrix
Gregg Braden

The Tao of Leadership
John Heider

The Tao of Pooh
Benjamin Hoff

Pooh and the Philosophers
John Tyerman Williams

The Miracle of Mindfulness
Thich Nhat Hanh

Maps to Ecstasy
Gabrielle Roth

The Prophet
Kahlil Gibran

The Book of One: the spiritual path of Advaita
Dennis Waite

The Bhagavadgita
Translated by Professor Vrinda Nabar and Professor Shanta Tumkur

The meditations of Marcus Aurelius
Emperor Marcus Aurelius

Encyclopaedia of Essential Oils
Julia Lawless

The Art of Aromatherapy
Robert Tisserand

The Herb Book
John Lust

Encyclopedia of Homeopathy
Dr Andrew Lockie

Index